THE
Complete
OWL

THE
Complete
OWL

Michael Leach

Photographs by Michael Leach

Chatto & Windus
LONDON

Published in 1992 by
Chatto & Windus Ltd
20 Vauxhall Bridge Road
London SW1V 2SA

A CIP catalogue record of this book is available from the
British Library

ISBN 0 7011 3786 X
Text copyright © Michael Leach 1992
Photographs © Michael Leach

Line illustration on page 36 by E.H. Shepard from
Winnie-the-Pooh copyright under the Berne Convention,
reproduced by permission of Curtis Brown Ltd, London

Drawings by Guy Troughton

Michael Leach has asserted his right to be
identified as the author of this work.

Colour separations and printed in Great Britain
by Butler and Tanner, Frome, Somerset

Frontispiece *Great grey owl*

Contents

Any resemblance or similarity to individual owls, living or dead, is purely intentional.

Acknowledgements

Recognition is due to many people who helped enormously in the production of this book. I would like to offer particular thanks to Jim Cooper; Mark Pilgrim and Roger Wilkinson of Chester Zoo; Nick and Tony Turk; John Burton; Ian Dean-Netscher; Keith Offord for his company, help and warm woolly hat; Peggy Jackson for her invaluable 'owl-sitting'; Robin Khan for advice on the text; Martin Danks for his unstinting veterinary expertise; Pat Sutton and Jeff Dalton of The Cotswold Falconry Centre; Dave Armitage of Banham Zoo in Norfolk; Rowena Skelton-Wallace at Chatto & Windus for all kinds of things; Guy Troughton for the drawings; Raymond Wilson for correcting my grammar; Colin Powell for his quick and efficient darkroom work; Ron Spillman for his photograph and, as always, my wife Judith for putting up with uncivilised hours, stained lampshades and caring for the owls that flit in and out of our lives.

Introduction

Man's fascination with owls has been recorded since the earliest times. Some people adore them and have owl ornaments in their living room, while others fear their presence and even their calls. Owls are worshipped as superior beings, or shunned for their supernatural powers. Owls have a well-defined position in the folklore of every country in which they live; and they can be found everywhere with the exception of the Antarctic and a few remote islands. There are more myths and beliefs about owls than there are about any other bird on earth.

Owls have an unmistakable place in the culture of the Western world. In the past, owl symbols were used simply as signs of good luck, but today they appear in anything from football club mascots to advertising aids. No self-respecting gift shop is without a display of owls made of shells, glass, pottery, wood or even polished coal, and many businesses have adopted the bird as their company logo, believing it to be a sign of their integrity and wisdom.

Assorted owl ornaments

The exposure to owls starts at a very early age. After bears, cuddly owls are one of the most popular of all childhood toys. They appear as important characters in numerous storybooks such as *Winnie the Pooh*, *The Sword in the Stone*, and as the 'elegant fowl' in Edward Lear's nonsense poem 'The Owl and the Pussycat'. The birds are portrayed either as the wise old owl who is all-seeing and friend to all, or as the witch's familiar who spies and carries out dirty deeds under cover of night.

There are two main reasons for our interest in the owl family. The first is that they look so very human; with their upright stance and lack of tail, they stand just like us. They don't dart about and flap their wings in the same way as other birds, they always seem to be composed and superior. But it is probably the owl's face that attracts us most, with its round head and earnest-looking expression. Owls have forward-facing eyes, something that few birds possess, and their narrow, curved beak is particularly nose-like. Some species look as if they are wearing glasses, which reinforces their 'wise' image; others even seem to have 'ears' in the right place.

Psychologists have known for a long time that most people have a special affinity for animals that have a similar physical appearance to humans. Koalas, pandas, bears and

The spectacled owl is a little-known species from South America – but is it 'wise'?

chimps are top of the popularity polls, while at the bottom are species that have too many legs, such as spiders, or not enough, like worms and snakes. Animals that are covered in scales or have beady little eyes also have few admirers.

Owls have all the right characteristics to make them attractive in our eyes, but their appearance is the result of evolutionary trial and error and has nothing to do with aesthetics. They are merely suitably equipped for their specialised way of life. But we, and I do include myself in this, are first drawn to them because they are visually appealing. Yet owls are normally seen for just a few seconds, whatever the situation. They stare with huge, penetrating eyes and then float off silently, returning to the secrecy of their own mysterious, private world.

This brings us to the second reason for the owl's appeal. They inhabit the night, a place that is unknown and alien to us. Under cover of darkness our own senses are too weak to gather accurate information about our surroundings. While the owl appears to fly effortlessly and without error, we stumble and trip. They catch running mice with ease and we have difficulty merely finding our way. Owls, therefore, have come to symbolise all that is mysterious about the night and their complete mastery of the darkness only shows up our own deficiencies. It is hardly surprising that we have endowed these birds with strange and supernatural powers.

Tawny owl waiting patiently for prey

My own first encounter with real owls came relatively late in life. Like everyone else, I had seen them from a long way off, hunting in fields at dusk, and had seen them fly through my headlight beams while driving late at night. I finally had the opportunity to see one at close quarters in my early twenties. At that time I was a starving naturalist living in South Devon, and I often went to my parents' home in Shropshire to stock up with good food. During one visit I was asked by a friend's next-door neighbour to take a parcel back to Devon. The package turned out to contain a tawny owl. The bird was about four months old and had been hit by a car shortly after leaving its nest for the first time. The left wing had been smashed and had had to be amputated. The local vet had done all he could and now the owl was going to be cared for by an expert who lived in a village just a few miles from me.

On the day I was to leave, the owl was delivered in a sturdy carrying box with plenty of breathing holes and thick bedding made of old towels. We set off and, as the train slowly meandered on the journey from Shrewsbury to Totnes, the owl and box sat safely behind my seat.

While not exactly tame, the tawny owl had come to tolerate humans during its convalescence. It made no noise and did not move around in its box, so I peered in every half-hour or so just to make sure that all was well. The owl dozed and rarely even looked up. Towards the end of the trip the train was held up for about ten minutes in a long tunnel and, like all the other passengers, I soon became impatient with waiting in the dark. Everything went very quiet – people always seem to talk more quietly than usual in the dark, and whispers and murmurs were the only sounds to be heard. Suddenly a long, tremulous hoot echoed around the silent, gloomy carriage. It was a young, inexperienced owl and the call was not all it should be. But it was still highly effective. The thin, wavy cry only lasted three or four seconds, and it utterly shattered the bored atmosphere. Directors of horror films always add the call of a tawny owl to soundtracks at tense moments, with good reason – it has to be one of the most evocative sounds in nature. Even after working with them for more than fifteen years, I can still see why the sound of these birds is described as 'spooky'.

There was a stunned silence for a few seconds, then a buzz of worried conversation sprang up everywhere. I feel certain that the second, more confident, longer hoot would have caused a riot if the train hadn't started to move at the same time. When we eventually pulled out of the tunnel and back into the security of sunshine, there was a collective sigh of relief; all was safe again and the owl resumed his silence and remained quiet for the rest of the trip. My fellow travellers obviously could not settle after the mysterious incident; the journey could not end too soon for any of us. And even now I can't help imagining people, over the brandy at dinner parties or after midnight when the lights are low, retelling their well-worn ghost story of a blood-curdling scream in a stranded train in the pitch black.

When I delivered the owl to its new home I found myself in a large garden full of cages. It was run by a retired teacher who took in and cared for injured owls until they could be returned to the wild. He introduced me to his charges: two more tawnies, each with a broken leg; a barn owl with a damaged eye and four young little owls that had been found, soaking wet, inside the hollow of a felled tree. I was hooked immediately and this accidental encounter was the start of a lifelong interest. I regularly went back to see them and the other owls that were constantly being brought into the sanctuary – it would have taken a harder man than I am to ignore the appeal of these birds.

My first experience of wild owls took place when I photographed a pair of tawnies nesting in an old oak tree on a neighbouring farm. From a strictly professional point of view, it seems that owls have been perfectly designed for photography. They are graceful, dramatic, beautiful and mysterious. I remember, on this occasion, sitting inside a small canvas hide built on a platform high in a nearby tree, waiting patiently for the return of the parents bringing in food for the three youngsters. I was using a lamp with a weak red bulb to throw some light on to the nest in front, and even without the owls, the scene looked decidedly eerie. Then suddenly, without warning, the owl was in front of me, carrying a wood mouse. It hesitated for a moment, dived inside the hole, emerged a minute later, then disappeared into the blackness.

During that visit I didn't take one photograph – I was so captivated with the silent appearance of the bird and the breathstopping feeling of being within arm's-length of a wild owl that all else was forgotten.

I have been a professional wildlife photographer and writer since the age of twenty-four and, although I have worked with many other subjects all over the world, my main love has always been owls. Looking back I suppose that the next stage was inevitable, but I was certainly surprised at the time. An unknown lady appeared at the door one day clutching a large cardboard box. 'I found this barn owl on the side of the road,' she said. 'Can you mend it please?'

I opened the box and there in the bottom, lying on its back with talons stretched out menacingly towards me, was a very angry tawny owl (I have since discovered that *any* owl is a barn owl unless proved to be otherwise). Judging by its active threats, there wasn't much wrong with this bird and I was surprised that anyone had managed to pick it up. Owls, particularly tawnies, are very capable of defending themselves and can inflict a lot of damage on the unwary. I put the owl into an empty shed and it sat for a few seconds, then exploded into flight, but it had no co-ordination or strength and quickly spiralled back to the floor with a crunch.

After a few telephone calls I found a genuine expert to examine the owl and he decided that the bird had probably been hit by a car and was suffering from temporary concussion. It needed to be fed well and kept quiet for a few days. I knew that the bird wouldn't do well on lean meat, because this lacks essential nutrients, so a more suitable food source had to be found. After a few more telephone calls I found a wholesale supplier of frozen mice and ordered a hundred. This particular owl was quite happy eating dead mice but, as I have found out many times since, few others are. The owl stayed with me for four days until it could fly strongly and was then released at the spot where it had been found. Each owl has its own territory; it needs to know the area intimately and defend it against rivals. To release an adult owl into an unsuitable or unknown habitat, or into the territory of another bird, could mean death to the freed bird.

From then on I regularly had cardboard boxes appear on my doorstep. In came owls that had been shot, poisoned or hit by cars. There were owls that had flown into overhead cables, become entangled in garden netting, been caught by cats, and even those that had got stuck down chimneys. Over the next few years I learned how to handle, force-feed and clean an owl without either of us getting hurt, although in the early days I received some very nasty puncture wounds from those awesome talons. Most of the casualties just needed time to recover from relatively minor injuries. After the initial examination, they were left undisturbed with plenty of food – this is the main treatment, even today.

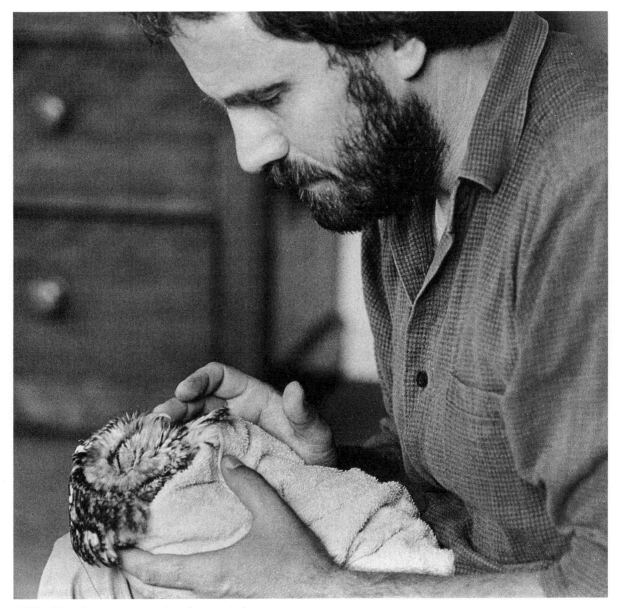

Michael Leach examing an injured tawny owl

Birds with more serious injuries are taken to a qualified veterinary surgeon, for they need expert medical attention if they are to have a chance of survival. Most vets admit that they have no previous experience in handling owls but are more than willing to try, and they have the surgical skills to repair all but the worst damage. I know of several that have a real interest and make no charge for their services when wild owls are involved.

Once the bird is fit and able to fly and hunt, it is returned to the wild. That moment of release makes all the effort worthwhile, but as the bird vanishes into the sky, I always wonder what will happen to it. Although the birds are ringed before they go, so far none have been found again. The average life span of a wild owl is remarkably short and very few die of old age. In fact, most of those we release will not last for more than three or four months. But if just a few survive long enough to breed once, then the effort has been justified.

One recent casualty was an ailing barn owl. It was a familiar story. A local electrician was driving home at eight o'clock in the evening when he saw a white shape suddenly materialise in front of his van. There was a slight bump and the mirage was gone. He stopped to have a look and from his seat he could see the owl lying about twenty feet away from the road. A vehicle travelling at 40mph can throw

Barn owl

a light object, like an owl, an awfully long way. The bird had fallen in a crumpled heap and its inert body convinced the driver that it was already dead, so he left it and drove on. As the miles passed he thought perhaps he should have checked to see if the owl really was beyond help. He therefore turned around and went back. This took about twenty minutes and when he reached the accident spot, the owl was still lying there, motionless. This was a minor miracle. Dead or injured animals do not last long at night, because they are normally taken by foxes, stoats or badgers.

Without looking closely at the bird, the man wrapped it in his coat and headed off again. Five minutes later the owl started to revive and by the time it reached me it was fully awake but couldn't stand up. Each time it tried it would teeter and then topple over. The owl had slight concussion but no other real damage. After eating several mice and proving it could stand up and fly properly, it was released.

In addition to the transitional owls that stay here for a short time to convalesce before going back to the wild, we have a small number that are residents. They cannot be released, either because they are too badly injured and could not survive in the wild, or because they have been hand-reared and are too tame to exist in a more natural habitat. We only keep owls as a last resort – whenever possible we make every effort to rehabilitate them but we are not always successful. Those that do stay here are found mates and are encouraged to breed so that their young can be released. Permanently disabled owls can never go back to the wild but, with a little luck, their offspring can lead a more normal life and contribute to the long-term survival of the species.

Owls face many natural dangers. They can die of various diseases, be eaten by larger predators, or die of hunger when the weather is bad or when the prey levels are low. Inevitably, it is man that poses the biggest threat. But for the actions of the human race, only a tiny number of species would face extinction instead of the twenty-five species that are now under real threat.

In ecological terms owls are no more – or less – important than any other group of animals – they are merely a small part of a complicated and interwoven network. Nevertheless, like so many other people, I do have a special regard for them. Much of this book is based on personal experience and my views may not always coincide with those of others. The study of animals is about interpretation and individual observation. Even within a single species there are differences in behaviour and, the longer I watch owls, the more obvious these become.

I should like this book to raise the general level of concern for owls and stimulate people so that they will build owl boxes, leave untouched wild areas as hunting grounds, think about pollution and the use of chemicals on the land, or possibly just join a conservation group. Owls are exciting birds and they are under direct threat because of us. Few wild animals can protect themselves from the effects of man and his treatment of the planet. Owls in particular need our help if we want our grandchildren to be able to catch a glimpse of their ghostly shapes floating silently through the skies of the twenty-first century and beyond.

Owl Facts

• Not all owls are nocturnal – some species, such as short-eared owls, hunt during the day.

• Unlike other birds' feathers, those of the owl have 'fringes'. These eliminate air noise, but also make flight less efficient.

• An owl's plumage is not waterproof and they absorb water like a sponge.

• In almost all species, there is no external difference between the sexes.

• Owls have a thin neck and extremely elastic muscles, which enable them to rotate their heads 180° in either direction.

• The right ear of a nocturnal owl is usually much bigger than the left. It is also normally placed higher on the head.

• An owl's legs are covered in feathers right down to the toes, which protects them from the teeth of prey and also keeps them warm during cold nights.

• The outside toe on each of an owl's feet is reversible – it can face either forwards or backwards.

• During a single night, an average tawny owl must eat eight mouse-size animals to sustain its energy levels.

• An owl has no teeth and cannot chew. It either swallows its prey whole or tears pieces off with its beak.

• Owls regurgitate undigested food – bones, teeth, fur and feathers – in cylindrical pellets.

• Owls rarely drink – they get most of the water they need from their prey.

• Many owls can hear their prey moving around underneath a covering of snow and will dive beneath the surface to catch it.

• An owl lacks even the most basic nest-building talent and will make its home instead in a 'pre-prepared' hole or an abandoned nest.

• Although the male owl is the more aggressive, the female is the stronger.

• During courting, a short-eared male will fly very high and clap its wings together so that the female can both see and hear it.

• There is an innate rivalry between the sexes and even while mating and feeding the young chicks, the male must approach the female with caution.

• Most species of owl usually pair for life while both partners are alive.

• Most owls roost in an upright position; the short-eared owl, however, roosts horizontally.

• Up to 40 per cent of owl chicks born in a single spring will be killed by road traffic before the following winter.

1 The Inside Story

In evolutionary terms, owls are probably perfectly adapted for their specialised life style. Their basic body-design has remained virtually unchanged since the Miocene period (ten to twenty-five million years ago), although there have been slight alterations and, as most evolution is a process that is too slow for humans to witness, it is possible that they are still developing in subtle ways which we do not appreciate. In fact, we know far less about the evolution of birds than we do about the much more ancient family of dinosaurs, mainly because of the lack of historical evidence.

Compared with giant reptiles, very few fossilised traces of birds have survived, for several reasons. First, the massive, dense skeletal remains of giant reptiles were not easily eaten by other animals, whereas birds are small and their fragile bodies would have been quickly disposed of by carrion eaters.

Second, dinosaurs often lived in or near water and after death, would have disappeared into mud – a perfect medium for creating fossils. Owls, on the other hand, evolved as woodland creatures and few would have lived near to coasts and estuaries, the areas that provided the necessary silt to preserve dead animals.

Third, reptile bones are heavy and relatively solid, much like our own; bird bones are very different. Instead of adopting the familiar hollow-tube type of structure, a bird's bone has evolved as a **honeycomb of tiny air sacs** strengthened with cross-struts. This is much less dense than a conventional mammal bone and keeps weight down to a bare minimum in order to let the bird fly. When the bird dies its bones simply disintegrate, with those that are not eaten eventually turning to dust in all but the most exceptional circumstances.

As there have been countless billions of birds, even though the chance of them being perfectly preserved might be low, it is safe to assume that a small number should have been successfully fossilised to tell the story of their evolution. Another problem remains,

The skeleton of a little owl shows the disproportionately large head that is common to all species

million years ago. Even when it is cleaned and laid out on a table, tangible evidence of ancient birds is often flimsy and difficult to decipher.

Excellent fossils have been found of early birds but even now there are gaps spanning millions of years that have not yet yielded worthwhile remains and we have to fill them using a mixture of logic and inspired guesswork. The evidence is still incomplete, but most people accept the theory that **birds evolved directly from reptiles**. The discovery of the small fossil known as *archaeopteryx* ('ancient wing') in Solnhafen, Germany, in 1860, was made the year after Charles Darwin published his *Origin of Species by Means of Natural Selection*.

The fossil is half-bird and half-reptile. This primitive animal had real teeth, something not found in birds today. Its forelegs could not be described as wings as they had claws and only crude feathers. Powered flight would have been impossible because the creature lacked the strong muscles needed to fly and its body was too heavy to be supported by rather weak wings. *Archaeopteryx* probably used its rudimentary wings to glide over short distances from tree to tree. It is not possible to say for sure if this was a direct ancestor of modern birds, for this species may have died out millions of years ago without leaving descendants. Although it is almost certain that the early birds must have closely resembled *archaeopteryx*, we will probably never

though: bird fossils are not as spectacular as those of large reptiles and mammals. A quarryman driving a bulldozer might not immediately recognise the vertebrae of a mammoth or the femur of a stegosaurus if they were unearthed by his machine, but he would certainly see them. Few people would notice the delicate tracery left by the outstretched wing of a relatively small bird that died ten

know exactly what evolutionary route they took to reach the form that we know today.

The first owls

The oldest distinct owl remains yet discovered date back to the Eocene period, about fifty million years ago. These were the *Protostrigidae* (first owls) and were similar in size and shape to the birds that we see now. The oldest on record has the scientific name *Protostrix* (first owl) *mimica* and comes from fossils found in Wyoming, USA. This long-dead bird resembled modern owls sufficiently for us to recognise it as a member of the same general family. To date, there is evidence of around fifty species that became extinct during prehistory. The oldest 'modern' species is the **long-eared owl**, which seems to have been in its present form for more than thirty-six million years. It is one of the most ancient of all bird species and dates back to the period when our own ancestors were undistinguished, ape-like creatures. Other early owls have been identified as fitting into the family groups of Bubo (eagle owls), and Strix (e.g. tawny, ural). There is still a great deal left to be learned about the evolution of owls.

One of the obvious questions to ask is 'What is an owl?' At first sight they seem to be much the same as hawks, eagles and falcons – the diurnal raptors, or birds of prey. Since they have hooked beaks and sharp talons, and share the same diet and hunting techniques, it is tempting to think that they are related. At one time zoologists classified all of these hunting birds together in one group. More recently they have been split into two very different orders (groups of related families); owls make up the Strigiformes and the daytime raptors fall into the order Falconiformes. They share similar characteristics because sharp, powerful talons are the most efficient weapon for catching small animals and a hooked beak is the most convenient, lightweight tool for tearing meat. The two groups may have shared a common ancestor somewhere in the distant past, but their parallel development is likely to be the culmination of countless evolutionary experiments within each group that independently solved the mutual problem of how to catch and eat animals in the best possible way.

The owl's nearest living relatives are a group known as the Caprimulgiformes. These are the strange **oilbirds**, **nightjars** and **potoos** that can be found on every continent except Antarctica. Often called goatsuckers, they are nocturnal birds that spend the daylight hours sleeping crouched on the ground or sitting motionless on a branch. At night they hunt in flight using their wide, gaping mouths as an aerial fishing net to catch small insects in the air. Nightjars are distantly related to owls and their nocturnal behaviour is a characterstic they both share.

This close-up of an eagle owl's feather shows the characteristic fringing that allows silent flight.

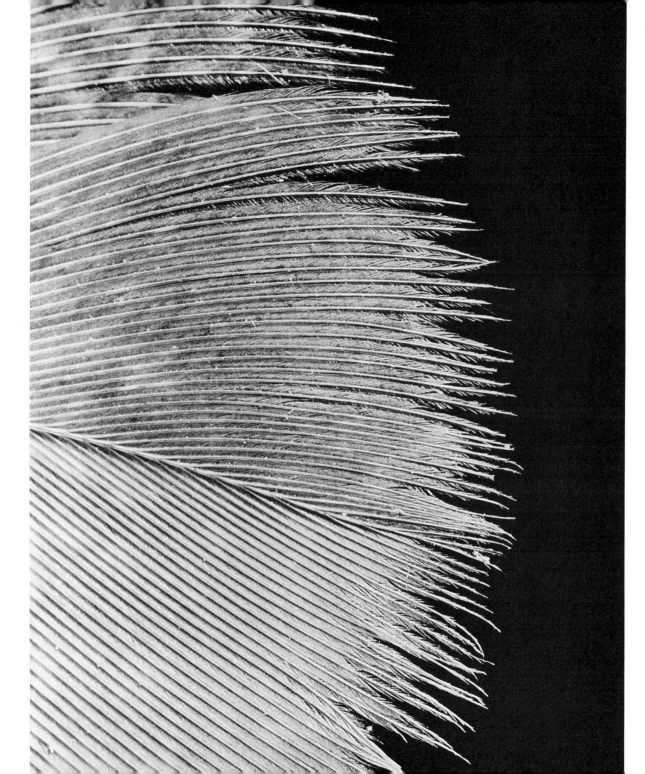

As with most owls, the long-eared's wings are large for its body size.

Feathers

The body of an owl is not unique: it has the basic, 'standard' design that all flying birds possess. Flight burns up a huge amount of energy, even for a lightweight bird, and requires a specialised anatomy. A bird's **pectoral muscles**, anchored on the keel-shaped **breastbone**, are the key to flight. It is these that drive the wings and supply the power for flying. These large muscles make up about 15 per cent of any flying bird's total weight and give it a broad-chested appearance. Arteries going from the heart to the flight muscles have a large capacity, and blood is pumped through them at high pressure, ensuring that there is a constant supply of oxygen to the bird's muscles.

Although the basic mechanics of flight are straightforward, owls do have some unique adaptations, the most interesting of which is the design of the feathers. The wings of all birds are made up of feathers of different sizes, each with its own function. For flight, the most important of these are the **primaries**, long, broad feathers at the end of each wing, which supply the lift and power that take a bird into the air. In a relatively large bird, the size of an average owl, primary feathers are long and stiff. When the bird flies, with wings flapping at full speed, the primary feathers are moving faster than any other part of the body. The sound effect is similar to the loud 'swishing' noise created by swinging a long stick around your head. The feathers of smaller birds 'whistle' as they fly and displace the air. This is unimportant for birds that eat fruit or seeds, but to an owl, which has to catch live prey, a noisy approach would be a major and possibly even a fatal handicap.

A feather is kept in shape by hundreds of tiny hooks known as **barbules**, which lock together and form a solid, blade-like structure with unbroken edges. On the leading edge of an owl's primary, however, there are no barbules; it is fringed and ragged. In flight, instead of the air passing around the edge of the feather, it passes through the fringe. The difference is tangible: conventional feathers are hard and smooth to the touch; owls have a soft plumage that feels more like velvet.

This feather structure gives owls a virtually soundless flight action. The first time that I realised the full effect of this was when a European eagle owl flew over my head. This is the largest species of owl in the world, with a wingspan of almost 1.8 metres. As it flew, the owl brushed my hair with its wingtips, but although I could feel the down-draught, I heard nothing as the bird sailed overhead on giant wings. There is something distinctly strange about watching such a huge bird move in complete silence. Another species of a similar size, such as a goose, would make enough noise to alert every small animal within fifty metres.

Although fringed feathers eliminate air noise, they also reduce flight efficiency, since the curious feather-design produces more drag and makes owls slower than they would be if equipped with ordinary plumage. To compensate a little for this, an owl's weight is very low for its wing size. Owls look bulky and heavy, but this is entirely due to their thick plumage; without feathers, the 'bald' bodies of most species would be less than half of their apparent size. The relationship between body weight and the size of the wings, which is known as wing-loading, governs the amount of effort needed for a bird to take off and fly. An average tawny owl has a weight (in kilogrammes) to wing area (square metres) ratio of about 3.5 to 1, while a similar-sized duck would be 10 to1. The higher the ratio, the harder a bird has to work to fly and the more noise it makes in the process.

An owl's wing-loading, therefore, is low, making flight almost effortless and economic in terms of the amount of energy required. It can turn and brake rapidly but, in a high wind, an owl is vulnerable to being tossed and carried as it lacks the weight and strength to fight strong air currents.

Owls' feather-design not only differs from other birds', it also differs between particular species. Not all species are totally nocturnal, and the **daylight-hunting owls** have less fringing on their feathers. The natural world is generally at its noisiest during the day and the sound of an approaching owl can be masked by birdsong and other strains of the countryside. The lack of fringing means that diurnal owls are faster and can manoeuvre more easily than their nocturnal counterparts. **Fishing owls** are the least concerned by noise as they specialise in taking prey directly out of a stream or lake. And, unlike the others, they have bald, scaly legs instead of the fine, thin feathers that cover the legs and feet of most owls. This makes their life easier when wading around in water.

Water, in the form of rain, is a very real problem for owls. The majority of birds use oil, from a gland beneath their tail, to give their feathers a waterproof coating which is regularly renewed during preening sessions. But whenever a group of animals evolve a highly specialised characteristic, there always seems to be a price to pay. Through natural selection, owls have unwittingly decided that silent flight is a more important survival aid than the possession of a waterproof plumage. The two cannot exist together. The oil that gives other birds their showerproof coat would clog up the fringes of an owl's feathers and the advantage of silence would be lost. In anything other than light drizzle, owls take to cover. Without the benefit of protected feathers, they absorb water like a sponge and quickly become too heavy to fly. In times of heavy rain, owls just have to wait for a break in the weather before they can hunt.

The owl's 'song'

An owl's plumage may be silent but owls can still be remarkably noisy when they choose to be. Among all the world's species there is a vast repertoire of calls that are used to communicate with potential mates and announce the ownership of a territory. The 'song' is recognised by other members of the same species and conveys definite messages.

The most familiar owl 'song' has to be the haunting, melodic 'kew-wick koooooo' cry of the tawny owl. Town-dwelling visitors to the countryside often complain that the cries of these very vocal birds keep them awake, but I must admit that I welcome them. The call of a

When wet, owls absorb water like a sponge. This tawny has just emerged from a bath.

Tawny owl at night

tawny owl is one of the most 'wild' and evocative in nature. I know of one lady who moved from the countryside into a town to be closer to the office where she worked. Three months later she moved back again because she 'missed the call of the owls' when she went to bed. According to several folklore experts this distinctive sound was believed to be responsible for the modern English name of the birds. The twin-syllable call was once interpreted as 'ow-wul' or 'yow-wul', which usage and time shortened to 'owl'. It is also likely that the word 'yowl' comes from the same source, the dictionary definition being 'long and loud cry of distress, especially of animals'.

It has to be said that not all owls make such a pleasant noise as the tawny. The **screech owl** of North America is well named, and I can believe that its less than attractive call would not always be welcome outside a bedroom window in the early hours. Some species do not even sound like owls. In South America the impressive **spectacled owl** is known locally as the **knocking owl** because its cry is so similar to the noise of a woodpecker tapping a tree. Also named because of their call are the **barking owl** and **laughing owl**, the latter being a small New Zealand species that is probably now extinct.

Owls that are active by day use their voices much less than their nocturnal relatives. In full light they can use visual contact and aerial displays to communicate with rivals and mates. Under the blanket of night, however, owls must use sound. With their keen sense of hearing, they can accurately identify all of the individual voices within earshot and any newcomer will quickly be noticed. If a strange owl is heard near the centre of an established range, the rightful owner will immediately arrive to drive away the interloper. Good human mimics can watch owls by copying their call and waiting until the angry resident homes in to evict the stranger.

A lot of the calling is to reinforce ownership of territory without coming to blows with rivals and many species of owl call just after dusk, before setting out to hunt. Within minutes they are answered from all around. This lays out the night's ground rules and each owl is aware of those areas that are already claimed. As long as each owl calls regularly, neighbours know that piece of land is still out of bounds, which prevents real trouble before it begins. The reverse must happen too. If a familiar call disappears for more than two or three nights, its absence is taken as a signal that an empty hunting ground is ready for occupation.

As they require less food, small owls have correspondingly smaller territories than the larger species. Because their neighbours are physically closer, the warning call does not have to travel far. This contrasts with giants like the **great grey** and **European eagle owl** which have deep, booming calls that echo around the landscape. Low-frequency

Male snowy owl on fence post

sounds travel further than those of high frequency, and these birds' calls can carry more than six kilometres.

Of course, there is an inevitable exception. The **flammulated owl** that lives on the western side of North America is one of the world's smaller species, yet its deep, powerful call sounds as if it should belong to a much larger bird. The monotonous cries have a unique ventriloquial quality and are extremely difficult to pin down. The carrying effect and unusually deep tones were highly perplexing to early ornithologists. After hearing the 'hoop hoop hoop' call, they could find the delicate flammulated owl but believed that they were looking for a much bigger bird, sitting somewhere else. The flammulated owl hunts over a far bigger range than other owls of similar size, so it has to have a voice that matches. An eagle owl can control a territory measuring up to 12.5 square kilometres. It takes a powerful call to cover that range.

Calls play an important part in the first stages of courtship, because male and female owls do not generally recognise each other by physical appearance. In almost all species there are no external differences between the sexes, as their plumage is identical. There are exceptions, such as the **snowy owl**, where the male is totally white and the female is white with chocolate-brown flecks, but even this can vary between individuals. In the majority of species the female is larger and heavier than her mate, but there are no precise size rules; large males and small females have both been recorded. And, unless the two are close together, the relative size is very difficult to judge. As owls have no usable sense of smell – and they look alike – they need to have some way of identifying each other. This is done through sound. In some cases it is simply a matter of the female being drawn to a male calling inside a territory that he has already claimed.

In other species the two birds sing a duet from different parts of the territory, forming a partial bond before they actually meet. **Spectacled owls** and **little owls** go through this procedure each year, but **eagle owls** are the most enthusiastic songsters of all. They can keep up a twin-noted call routine for several hours; and they are not always too concerned about the identity of their partner.

I've always found that the European eagle owl is the most susceptible to good imitation. It only takes a little practice to master the 'ooo-hooo' call and, if there is an eagle owl nearby, it should answer within minutes.

There are two more types of sound produced by adult owls. The first is a rapid clicking, known as **beak-snapping**, which is used as a defensive warning when they are challenged by a rival or enemy. In the larger owls, the snapping is often used with a full visual display, which is very dramatic. The wings are drawn forward and out, each feather is raised, both eyes are opened wide and, if they have them, the ear tufts are lifted. This makes the bird look much bigger and the overall effect is daunting – an extremely effective warning signal. Most species also have an irritated **hiss**, which is used when they are surprised or disturbed but not really frightened. It is not a true threat of violence, more a signal to keep away.

2 Owl Lore

It really is remarkable that so many varied and contradictory beliefs can surround the small, secretive family of owls. The birds themselves may not be seen by many people but stories about them abound.

Modern myths fall into two camps, the most powerful being the ill-omen theory. Shortly after moving into my house, I gave a talk on owls in the local village hall and took along a tame owl, which was duly admired. Before I left, several people stopped to say how interested they had been to see the bird, but added that they were very pleased that our house was isolated and that their own homes were well out of earshot of my garden and the sound of its doom-laden birds.

This fear of an owl's call is deep seated and dates back countless centuries. In *Henry V*, Shakespeare wrote, 'The owl shrieked at thy birth, an evil sign', summing up the mistrust of the unseen bird and its mournful cry.

The other view of owls is almost exactly the opposite; owls are portrayed in popular literature as noble and benign birds, but above all they are wise. This concept is captured in an anonymous but frequently quoted rhyme:

> A wise old owl sat in an oak,
> The more he saw the less he spoke,
> The less he spoke the more he heard,
> Why can't we all be like that bird?

I hate to be the bearer of bad news, but it has to be said that owls are not exactly the brightest birds in the world. In fact, on a league table of intelligence, owls come a long way down, particularly when compared with the masterminds of the bird world, such as crows and parrots. Owls are supreme in the techniques required for survival but their intellectual skills are lacking.

It is extremely difficult to assess accurately an animal's intelligence, or even to draw up a fair definition of the word. One widely accepted way of measuring brain power is to analyse how an animal reacts and adapts to completely new circumstances. This is just a

Barn owl, looking serene and 'wise'

rule of thumb and has lots of loopholes, but it works adequately for most species. Many of the world's most intelligent animals are highly adaptable and quickly learn to alter their behaviour to suit changing conditions. They are quick to seize opportunities to exploit new food supplies or breeding grounds.

In-depth research shows that owls cannot easily or quickly adapt their behaviour. While this is not the only criterion for judging intelligence, it strongly suggests, when taken with other evidence, that owls are not the wise old birds of myth. Even I, with a self-confessed and boundless enthusiasm for the entire family, have to say that owls are not the most mentally agile creatures that I have ever met.

Greek myths

Tales of the owl's reputed intelligence go back thousands of years. Throughout history man has attempted to interpret and explain the owl's behaviour, and some of the theories are highly ingenious.

One of the first documented owl references comes from the early Greek civilisation, where gods were the absolute rulers. They controlled weather, emotions, animals and life itself. With such awesome power, mortals had to treat them with great respect, worship them and build elaborate tributes to their glory if their wrath and vengeance was not to rain down upon the lesser beings below.

The sophisticated Greek city of Athens derives its name from the Goddess of Prophecy and Wisdom, Pallas Athene. Like all deities she had underlings to carry out her wishes and they often appeared in animal form. Her special messengers were the owl, and not just any owl, but the one that we now call the **little owl**. These birds nested inside cavities in the walls of the Acropolis, containing the temple of Athene, and the locals soon realised that the Goddess must have approved of the owls to allow their presence inside her sanctuary.

Because of their close relationship with a major god, these owls were held in high esteem. The early Greeks thought that their bright yellow eyes were magic and enabled them to see at night. When Athene had coins minted in her honour, one side portrayed the Goddess herself, the other showed the omnipresent owl. Athenian slang referred to the coins as 'owls'. Everyone knew that Athene could transform herself into a little owl at will and, in this disguised form, would fly about the countryside to look at her subjects without being noticed.

In 490BC there was a battle at Marathon between the Greeks and Persians. The Greek soldiers were dangerously outnumbered and quickly losing ground when a little owl flew over the field of battle. The tired soldiers were overjoyed to see that their Goddess had appeared to help them in their hour of need. With a burst of strength and confidence, the Greeks drove their enemies back to their ships. The owl's appearance proved to be so

Greek tile showing the highly esteemed little owl

effective that devious Greek generals used secretly to carry captive little owls into battle, releasing them if things started to go badly.

Little owls bred freely in all the stone buildings of Athens; the protection of the Goddess made them safe from human persecution and they enjoyed an undisturbed existence. The modern scientific name for the little owl is *Athene noctua*, Athene's owl, and this association with the Goddess of Wisdom is the most likely explanation for the first stories about the owl's supposed intelligence.

The ancient Greeks must have been a partisan bunch when it came to birds. They revered the little owl, but were much less enthusiastic about the **long-eared owl**. These particular birds were thought to be unbelievably stupid. Greeks used to say that if a human found a long-eared owl in daylight it would not fly away, just sit and look. Should the human then keep walking around the owl, it still wouldn't leave but would carefully watch the circling figure, keeping its body motionless but rotating its head slowly round and round until it strangled itself. The Greek word for long-eared is *Otus*, which today is the scientific family name for screech and scops owls, but which the ancient Greeks used as an insult to be hurled at someone when their intelligence was in doubt.

Omens of doom

The Greeks' appreciation of little owls contrasted sharply with the view that was then held by the rest of the world on owls in general. Virtually every early reference to owls speaks of them as omens of doom and death. Sometimes the myths are contradictory. One early Christian tale says that owls had sweet, melodic voices until one witnessed the crucifixion of Christ, after which they adopted a dull funereal hoot as a sign of deep mourning.

A rather better-known tale tells of the time when Jesus was hungry and had no money for food. He went into a baker's shop and asked for bread. The baker's generous wife prepared some dough for the oven but her daughter appeared and complained to her mother that she was giving too much away. The daughter insisted that only half the amount should be used, so her mother obeyed and cut the dough. Immediately, the half-piece doubled in size. The miserly daughter was astonished and called out 'heugh, heugh', and then promptly turned into an owl.

Owls are mentioned several times in the Bible but their appearance does depend upon the version that you look at. The Authorised Version translates the original phrase *bath yannah* into 'owl', while the Revised Standard Version interprets it as 'ostrich'. There is yet more confusion when one refers to 'great owl', while the other talks about an ibis. In Leviticus (ch.11, v.17) the great owl and little owl are condemned as 'unclean', as carrion eaters whose flesh is an abomination and not to be consumed by humans.

Hebrews believed that owls harboured the returned soul of Lilith, first wife of Adam, whose call brought death and destruction to anyone within earshot. Amulets against her – and the owls '– power were worn until the Middle Ages. This superstitious fear dates back to early Egypt, where owls were messengers from the underworld, treacherous birds of death and coldness.

The idea that the call of an owl foretold imminent death was widespread. Three Roman Caesars, including Julius, were warned of their fate by the daytime cries of an owl. Commodus Aurelius is reputed to have met a screech owl that had accidentally strayed into his rooms and this proved to be fatal, as he died just a few hours later.

If the myths are anything to go by, Romans were terrified of owls and held them in awe. They became almost obsessed by the fear of hearing a call and if a Roman saw an owl, it was to be killed before it could cry out with a death sentence that could not be avoided. Pliny the Elder, a doubtful ornithologist at the best of times, wrote, 'The owl betokeneth always some heavy news and is most execrable and accursed in presaging public affairs . . . If he be seen either within cities or abroad in any place, it is not for good, but prognosticates some fearful misfortune.'

It is easy for us to mock such beliefs from the scientific, rational safety of the twentieth century, but much of nature was a closed book in Roman times. In those days, darkness was inexplicable, dangerous and dirty, and any animal that shied away from the sun and moved confidently under the cloak of night had obviously allied itself to the powers of evil.

The influence of the powerful Roman culture spread throughout Europe and North Africa and is felt even today, when superstitions that began more than 2000 years ago still abound. Many are just variations on the same theme: for example, it is well known that anyone who looks into an owl's nest will become depressed and morose for life; and that if an owl lands on the roof of a house, then someone within will die before the next sunset. The Hindu religion once insisted that if an owl was seen to land on top of a house, the whole roof should be dismantled and replaced.

Some myths are a little more obscure and difficult to understand. In Wales, the hoot of an owl proclaimed the fact that an unmarried girl had lost her virginity. Anyone who has ever walked through a Welsh valley in autumn cannot fail to find this notion startling, for all around, almost non-stop, are the calls of tawnies echoing across the landscape. In France, a call heard by a pregnant woman meant that the baby would be a girl. Parts of China believed that the image of an owl on each corner of a roof would ward off lightning. The mythology of some North

American Indians held that owls were not the cause, but simply messengers, of doom. Hearing a call heralded death unless the listener responded immediately by imitating the owl's mournful sound. In this way death could be fended off.

Genghis Khan, the twelfth-century Mongol warrior, was once fleeing from a band of enemies, but was outnumbered and needed a place to hide. Eventually, he found a thick copse of trees, where he and his men sat silently. Very soon, an owl appeared and sat on a tree at the edge of the wood. When the opposing forces saw the bird, they knew that Genghis and his men couldn't be there if the owl sat so peacefully. They therefore moved away and the Mongols escaped. Genghis Khan then adopted the owl as a good luck charm – from then on he and his followers wore owl feathers and charms both to protect themselves from danger and pay tribute to their special saviour.

A Brazilian legend also holds the owl in high esteem. In South America there is a large member of the rodent family called a coypu. It looks just like a big, slightly round, rat, and it has bright orange teeth. Although they were, and still are, not welcomed because of their habits of eating crops and undermining riverbanks with their endless tunnels, the coypu had one saving grace – its

Barn owls are appropriately named, for they like to nest and roost in old buildings

fine fur was highly prized and could be sold for a considerable price. Once their financial value was realised, random killing of coypus became illegal because no one wanted to wipe them out. Slowly, the coypu population grew and some were forced to move to other areas in search of food and living space. The bolder ones entered the city of Buenos Aires, where their numbers eventually reached levels that terrified the residents. Without warning a huge flock of owls arrived and wiped out the invading coypus, saving the city from the twin menace of subsidence caused by tunnelling and the destruction of food supplies in the wake of the insatiable rodents.

Witches' familiars and ghosts

Most stories prefer to dwell on the supposedly sinister aspects of owls. In the sixteenth and seventeenth centuries it was widespread knowledge that owls were the familiars of witches and there was a strong rumour that the Devil himself kept one as a pet.

Occasionally it is not human fancy that begins the stories; it can be the owls themselves that are responsible. For centuries European folklore has related stories about souls of the departed that are tied to the earth, restlessly wandering the land where their mortal remains lie. Tales of ghosts in graveyards are one of the most common, and earliest, themes in our supernatural literature. Returning souls is one explanation, but there is another that is more realistic.

In flight the white under-feathers of the barn owl are clearly visible

In all cultures, burial grounds are holy or at least highly respected places which, by tradition, are not disturbed. These patches of land therefore become quiet havens, even when in the centre of a town. Trees and flowers are planted as marks of respect and slowly a new type of habitat emerges. As a wildlife reserve it is almost perfect since the world's most dangerous and destructive animal, man, is a rare and subdued visitor. Invertebrates, butterflies and wild flowers thrive and multiply – and so do mice and voles. The abundance of prey quickly attracts predators; stoats, weasels and foxes are frequent hunters in churchyards but their dark, earthbound bodies are not easily seen. Barn owls are an altogether different matter. The white feathers of their chest and underwings can be clearly seen on all but the very blackest night.

Anyone who has ever watched a hunting **barn owl** will have no difficulty imagining the scene when a lone walker passes a quiet graveyard around midnight. Glancing around, he sees a faint white shape silently floating towards him, gliding effortlessly over the tops of the ancient graves. The barn owl is out on a hunting flight, keeping close to the grass, looking for small animals.

One of the better understood aspects of the phenomenon of optical illusion is that very light objects always look bigger than they really are when seen in the dark. At night, barn owls in flight can seem to be truly massive – and even ghost-like – when their broad wings reflect the moonlight.

Some owls have pleasant soothing calls, but not the barn owl. It was once known as the screech owl and this is still an understatement, for barn owls give out an unearthly shriek that would not be out of place in a horror film. It is not meant as a warning call, it is simply for communication, but their cry really does sound as if it comes from a tormented soul. Even those passers-by who carried a lamp were not immune, for the reflection off the owl's eyes looks bright red at night.

Anyone who witnesses the pale shape of a hunting barn owl, with its piercing scream, hovering over an empty graveyard, will be in little doubt about what he has seen. The ghostly appearance and suitably eerie call of these owls must have convinced generations of superstitious folk that spirits rise at night and haunt their graves. As the tale was retold, the facts would become enhanced; the figure would grow larger and more menacing, its eyes glow scarlet with the flames of hell as the strange unearthly figure hovered above the ground.

The barn owl's association with graveyards probably helped perpetuate the myth about all owls being portents of death. In Germany the tawny owl's 'kew-wick' call has been taken to mean 'komm mit' – 'come with me' – and was always supposed to be heard just after death, when the owl collects the departed soul. As far as the owls themselves were concerned these beliefs were harmless and irrelevant, but many superstitions were certainly not. Throughout Europe, everyone knew that a dead owl nailed to your door was a strong defence against evil. This single conviction must have been the cause of mass destruction of owls and there were many more in the same vein. Every warrior needed to carry an owl's heart into battle to provide extra courage. When used in conjunction with the bird's right foot, an owl's heart tucked in a man's left armpit was a potent antidote for the bite of a rabid dog. At least, it was in Germany. In America, if the same combination was laid on to the chest of a sleeping man, he could then be asked any question and could not help but reply truthfully.

Owls and folk medicines

Various parts of an owl's anatomy were highly prized as ingredients for folk medicines. One much-acclaimed cure for gout called for the sufferer to 'take an owl, pull off her feathers, salt her well for a week, then put her into a pot, and stop it close, and put her into an oven so that she maybe brought into a mummy'. This was then finely mashed, mixed with pig grease and smeared liberally on to the affected place.

Owl eggs were just as popular, when used in the right way of course. Given to a drunk, they forced him to give up his intemperate ways for ever. In a soup, taken only when the moon wanes, they were a sovereign cure for epilepsy. The entire body of an owl could be made into a soup if whooping cough was the problem. Baked and powdered feet were an excellent potion if the patient had been bitten by a snake. Due to the owl's ability to see in the dark, powdered owl eyes were widely accepted as a quick way to improve a human's eyesight. In parts of India, owl meat was a strong aphrodisiac. Fortunately, these practices have all died out, but the **collared scops owl** from Asia is still much sought after as a vital ingredient in a home-made cream that fights rheumatism.

North American Indians had a much more sensible and admirable attitude to owls. Owls were respected for their skill and stealth. The Creek Indians thought that the **great horned owl** was an earthly contact with the spirit world. Only the medicine man could communicate with these birds and this gave him a direct line to the gods. To confirm this position, he wore a stuffed horned owl as a hat. He must have felt it worthwhile, for these are big birds and moving around cannot have been easy. To increase their status, medicine men often hand-reared young owls in secret. When the passive adult owl was produced later, its friendliness was further proof of the power of the medicine man. Hopi Indians looked on burrowing owls as the benign keepers of dead souls that dwelt in underground tunnels.

The mythology surrounding owls is endless; as a group, they have stirred up the fertile imagination of countless storytellers. The fourteenth-century *Legend of Good Women* by Chaucer tells of 'The owle al night about the balkes word, that prophet is of wo and mischaunce'. William Shakespeare used the owl as a powerful symbol in many of his plays, often at the most dramatic moments. In *Macbeth*, when the three witches conjure up their magic potion, the recipe calls for 'Lizard's leg and howlet's wing, / For a charm of powerful trouble'; and following the murder of the king, Macbeth says, 'I have done the deed.

A barn owl searching for food in a churchyard – the start of another ghost story?

Dids't thou not hear a noise?', to which Lady Macbeth answers, 'I heard the owl scream.'

In France, eagle owls are known as *hibou grand duc*, the grand-duke owl. During the Middle Ages there were rigid rules of dress: no one with a status lower than a duke was allowed to wear erect feathers in his hat. It was soon noticed that the generously tufted eagle owl had the same exclusive headwear as the French nobility and it was afforded the same respect. Other eared owls were similarly honoured – , long-eareds were *hibou moyen-duc* (middle duke) and the tiny scops was *hibou petit-duc* (little duke).

This habit of endowing animals with human characteristics is thoroughly frowned upon by scientific purists. It is wrong to view any other species and its behaviour by the emotions and conventions of our own lives. Nevertheless it is at this level that most people first form their opinion of any animal. We like owls for their cuddly appearance but feel that their predilection for eating little furry animals is somehow not quite 'nice'. This is a very common reaction when an unenlightened viewer watches an owl swallow a whole mouse for the first time. Along with so many other species of animal, all through our shared history, owls have suffered terribly from superstition stemming from Man's ignorance.

'And if anyone knows anything about anything,' said Bear to himself, 'it's Owl who knows something about something,' he said, 'or my name's not Winnie-the-Pooh,' he said.

A. A. Milne, *Winnie-the-Pooh*

Merlyn took the Wart's hand and said kindly, 'You are only young, and do not understand these things. But you will learn that owls are the politest and most courteous, single-hearted and faithful creatures living. You must never be familiar, rude or vulgar with them, or make them look ridiculous.

T. H. White, *The Sword in the Stone*

3 Super Senses

Although every non-zoological reference to owls shows them as being exclusively nocturnal creatures, there are a small number of species, such as the **short-eared** and the **hawk owl**, that are just like us; they are active in daylight and sleep at night. Others, such as the **snowy** and **great grey owl**, live close to the Arctic Circle, where the number of daylight hours varies throughout the year from zero to twenty-four, depending on the season. In the summer months they have to hunt in daylight because there is no real night, while in mid-winter it is permanently dark. Finally, I once watched a **little owl** hunting on a rocky mountainside in southern Spain at two o'clock in the afternoon. It was early June and the temperature was a scorching 32° C. Most owls, however, are truly **nocturnal**. They all appear to have originally evolved for this kind of life style and those species that have strayed from the ways of their ancestors seem to have adopted their behaviour in relatively recent times.

Everything about an owl's physiology is suited to a night-time existence but there are still many inaccurate myths which try to explain their prowess in the dark. Most date back to a time when no scientific data existed to explain just how the owl hunted in, what seems to us, pitch-black conditions. The zoological facts, though, are no less fascinating than the supernatural explanations that preceded them.

Eyesight

The most widespread and persistent beliefs concern the owl's eyesight. Extraordinary claims have been made about its ability to see at night, and I would just like to lay aside some of the more common myths: owls do not see by infra-red light and neither can they use sonar, like bats. And despite rumours to the contrary, owls can see perfectly well in daylight; their eyesight is approximately the same as ours in bright sunshine and some can see better than we can, although their colour vision is not as good. Another misconception is that sunlight hurts their eyes. Without suit-

The diurnal short-eared owl

able protection, it is true that the owl's sensitive retina could be damaged by bright light, but even the most nocturnal of species have effective built-in screens for protection.

The first line of defence is the **pupil**, which can close to a mere dot to cut down the light passing into the eye. In very bright conditions, owls can also use their **'third eyelid'**, which is more properly known as a **nictitating membrane**. This is an all-purpose device that helps protect the eye and keep it clean and the membrane is transparent in most birds. An owl's, though, is slightly opaque, appearing as a blue-grey colour when the bird blinks, which helps to deflect high-intensity light.

Eye position

It is possible to guess, with some accuracy, whether an animal is basically a predatory or prey species by looking at the position of its eyes. Small birds that eat seeds or insects are vulnerable to a wide range of enemies. To allow them to see as much approaching danger as possible they have eyes on either side of their head, giving a very wide field of view; the only blind spot is directly behind. In some species, such as the woodcock, the angle of view is 200° in each eye. The two overlap, so these birds can see what is happening in front, to the side and behind, all at the same time. Although this is an excellent early-warning system, the quality of sight suffers. The image received by each eye is distorted and two-dimensional. This is not a problem for a bird that finds food by probing mud with its beak; but it would be for a bird of prey that needs to judge accurately the exact position and distance of a moving animal in order to survive.

All birds of prey have eyes that can look forward, but these are usually situated on the 'corner' of their heads to provide good front and side vision. The position of an owl's eyes is the same as that of a human's, on a flat face with both looking directly forward. To gauge distance we need perspective and this is provided by a three-dimensional image that can only be achieved by having two eyes looking at the same object simultaneously. Each eye

White-faced scops owl showing nictitating membrane

sees a slightly different image and when the owl unconsciously puts the two together, it can judge the exact distance with astonishing accuracy. An owl's eye has a field of around 110°, but their combined binocular vision is 70°. This is more than any other bird and, as far as we can tell, owls have the best range-

Tawny owl

finding skills in the bird world.

It is a fundamental physical law that the stereoscopic effect is improved as the distance between the eyes increases. This is one reason why an owl has a 'flat' face, as it allows the largest possible eye separation. Large species have well-spaced eyes, so they have a good three-dimensional picture of the world around them. The smaller species are less fortunate because their eyes are closer together. To compensate for this, **little owls**, **burrowing owls** and all the small-headed species weave their heads quickly from side to side and rapidly bob up and down when they spot prey or a possible enemy. This gives a series of slightly different sightings that can be put together to form one highly detailed, 3-D image.

I once had a telephone call late one evening from a worried farmer who said that he had found an injured tawny owl lying on the side of the road. I went to investigate. Half an hour later I was shown into a warm farmhouse kitchen where the owl had been left undisturbed in a cardboard box. When I looked inside, instead of seeing a tawny owl, there was the saddest-looking little owl that I had ever seen. These birds may be tiny but they are tough, gritty and have plenty of spirit. Although smaller than a man's hand, a healthy little owl normally has no hesitation in attacking any human who has the nerve to put him in a cardboard box.

This owl was not in the mood to attack anything. Although he was standing on his feet, the front of his head was resting on the floor. He was virtually bent double, a contortion I have never seen an owl perform before or since. When he saw me, instead of backing into a corner and extending his talons, this little owl tiredly flopped on to his back, his dull, glazed eyes taking little notice of what was happening around it. By the look of the injuries, he had been hit by a car. There was blood trickling from his nostrils and beak and both eyes were half closed. Even while I examined him, there was no reaction at all from the little bird. This is always a bad sign.

At home, the owl was left inside the box overnight, in the warmth and quiet of our living room. I did not really expect him to be alive in the morning. No matter how many times it happens, the death of a rescued owl is always depressing and it was with a heavy heart that I opened the box before breakfast the following morning. In the corner, wheezing slightly, snapping his beak, with both eyes glaring out at me, was an unbowed little owl. He was aggressive and angry, and now had a good chance of recovery.

Of all the owls that I have ever handled, little owls seem to adapt most quickly to temporary captivity. Within twenty-four hours, this one was still hostile but eating heartily. The bleeding had stopped and he quickly got down to the job of cleaning his feathers. But we soon noticed that something was wrong. While his left eye remained brilliant yellow, the other grew dark and discoloured. There was a way we could check if the eye was still in working order. The pupils of all owls should respond very quickly to changes in light levels and with a bright torch, we could see that the left pupil reacted instantly because it shrank down to a mere dot. The right one, however, remained stubbornly open.

A day later, small wrinkles appeared on the surface of the right eyeball. A visit to Martin Danks, our vet who has a special knowledge of owls and birds of prey, confirmed our suspicion. Our little owl was now blind in one eye. The eyeball was completely dead; the blood supply had been cut off as a result of the accident. That eye could see nothing and, if it was left in place, would start to decompose and the owl would certainly die of blood poisoning.

That afternoon the vet took out Spock's (our name for the new owl) right eye and stitched the lids together. It was the first such operation that Martin had ever done and the outcome was uncertain. I took the owl home in a cardboard box, lined with an old but clean shirt. After two hours he started to twitch and then sleepily opened his remaining eye. Within six hours of coming out of the anaesthetic, Spock was on his feet and eating again. The operation had been a complete success.

Spock was the most endearing owl I have ever known. During convalescence he stayed indoors, something no other patient has ever been allowed to do. When the house was quiet, Spock sat on the windowsill watching the world go past. When visitors came he liked to sit on their heads, pull up one thick leg into his feathers and go to sleep. (This singular honour was not always appreciated, as owls cannot be house-trained.)

Spock did not even try to fly for two or three days after the operation, but when he did, the results were disastrous. It is quite easy to guess where an owl is aiming for, as it spends a long time looking at the landing site before take-off. On his first post-operative flight, Spock eyed the top of the bookcase carefully with his perpetual wink – and took off. He completely missed it. Instead of landing delicately on the wooden rail he sailed over and crash-landed behind. A few seconds later he totally missed landing on top of the television and saved himself only by scrabbling frantically at the new curtains behind with his sharp claws. Without the use of two eyes, he had lost all idea of perspective and could no longer judge distances. Sometimes he would overshoot his chosen perch, while at other times he would try to land too early, in mid-air. The poor owl must have been thoroughly confused and it took several weeks for him to conquer the difficulty.

To fix the landing point precisely he could only use his one good eye, and he had to learn a new technique. He bobbed much higher and lower, and weaved further from side to side, than would any less disadvantaged owl. In this way his one eye was taking as many different sightings as two would normally take. Within a month of losing his eye, Spock could fly and land almost perfectly.

Eye structure

To appreciate the suitability of the owl's eyes for the bird's life style, it is useful to understand the basic workings of an eye. Except in deep caves, the natural world never experiences absolute darkness. Even on the blackest night there is always light present, but we cannot detect it simply because we don't have the right visual equipment. The most prominent feature about an owl's eyes is the sheer size – for instance, those of a **European eagle**

Spotted eagle owl

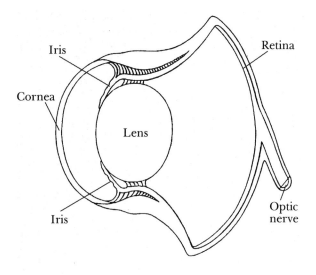

Typical owl eye design

owl are bigger than our own. Like a lens or a window, large eyes let through more light than small ones. The cornea is unusually large in owls, allowing the maximum amount of light to reach the **retina**, the layer of cells at the back of the eye that detects light and sends signals to the brain.

Owls' eyes have totally different proportions from those of other birds and are even further removed from our own. If our optical system and eye-to-skull proportions followed those of an owl, our heads would have to be the size of a barrel to accommodate our eyes. If the owl's eyes followed the usual bird pattern, with its small cornea, they would have to be even larger to focus incoming light on to the retina.

The massive size and odd shape of an owl's eyes make any kind of independent movement impossible – an owl's eyes cannot turn in any direction within the skull. To compensate for this, owls have developed an exceptional ability to **swivel their heads** rather than their eyes. An owl's neck appears to be thick and powerful, but looks are misleading, for the neck is in fact thin and scrawny, and the bulk is simply made up of feathers. The thin neck and elastic muscles enable owls to rotate their heads all the way round. When looking forward, they are in the resting position, halfway through the possible rotation; they can then look directly behind by swivelling their head 180° in either direction.

Once inside the eye, light is detected by sensitive cells in the retina at the back. There are two different designs of cell, known as rods and cones, because of their shape. Cones operate in bright light and provide fine detail and colour vision, while rods work in much lower levels of light but lack sharp definition and colour perception. An average sunny day can be ten million times brighter than a dark night, so it is hardly surprising that the eyes of nocturnal and diurnal animals differ. Human eyes are not particularly efficient at gathering light – they do not need to be because of the abundance of light during the day. Much of the light that enters our eyes passes straight through the retina without triggering any of the sensitive cells. But enough is still picked up to give us excellent vision. Our own retina is made up mainly of cones, so we have good colour vision and high resolution but lack of good night-sight.

Owls, like all truly nocturnal animals, have the opposite arrangement. They do possess cones, but the owl's retina is made up primarily of rods. This gives the birds excellent low-light vision but, probably, imperfect colour perception. (Colour sight is very difficult to test in animals; we do know that owls can see strong, bright colours but they appear to get mixed up between dark reds, dark greens and grey.)

All nocturnal animals have a mirror-like surface, called a tapetum, behind the retina. This picks up the light that has missed the layer of sensitive cells and reflects it straight back through the retina again. This second pass increases the likelihood of most of the light entering the eye being detected and used. It is this reflective layer that produces the characteristic eye-shine that makes an owl's eyes look bright red when they are caught in the headlights of a car.

A further advantage, within the eye itself, is the huge degree of change possible in the pupil size. During the day, the pupil closes down to a mere dot, but at night it opens up enormously to allow in the maximum amount of light. In species such as the **long-eared owl**, which has a bright orange iris in daylight, the pupil becomes so large at night that the surrounding colour virtually disappears. This effect is very rarely seen by

Owls can rotate their heads in any direction. This tawny is looking directly upwards, something they very rarely do.

humans because, as soon as the owl encounters bright light, the pupil instantly closes and the coloured iris reappears.

Tawny owls appear to have the most advanced night sight, and can detect dead prey in conditions that look pitch black to a human. It is possible that their eyesight is a hundred times more sensitive than our own in the dark. The tiny **European pygmy owl** is not quite as accomplished. Its eyes are only half as good as ours: in the half-light of dusk a pygmy owl could not see a mouse that would be clearly visible to a human with only average sight. But as pygmy owls hunt in daylight, they do not need perfect night vision. Their eyes are good enough to allow them to find food, and that is all they need.

There is still some argument between experts over just how well owls can see at night. The truth is that we will probably never really know how an owl views the nocturnal world. We do know that the combination of large eye-size, tapetum and high sensitivity gives them good performance in low-light but it is not good enough to locate prey in the near-absolute darkness of a dense conifer woodland that would be encountered by a great grey owl hunting voles.

Hearing
Following centuries of misdirected folktales and supernatural beliefs about owls' ability to catch animals in the dark, we now know that their eyesight is not infallible, because it is not the only sense that they use to find prey, and is probably of secondary importance for those species that are totally nocturnal.

Owls have an astonishingly accurate sense of hearing that plays a vital role in gathering information. Their ears are designed to pick up and concentrate upon the slightest sound that might betray the presence of a feeding animal. Although many owls, like the mis-

leadingly named **long-eared**, look as if they have ears on top of their head, the real organs are well hidden beneath their thick feathers. External ear flaps would cause drag during flight so, like all birds, an owl's ears are simply holes in the skull. The 'eared owls' (less than a third of the world's species) have tufts of long feathers that are used only for display. When the owl is relaxed, these feathers lie back on top of the skull; when the bird is alert or feeling aggressive, they become erect. Tufts also help to break up the owl's silhouette when roosting in a tree, making it more difficult to see. These plumes have nothing to do with hearing and do not contain anything but feathers and this causes understandable confusion for the casual observer as the tufts are situated exactly where he would expect ears to be.

Eyesight is the most important sense for ordinary **diurnal birds**, which all have acute vision and good colour-sensitivity; for them, hearing is a secondary warning system that is used mainly to detect potentially dangerous movements hidden from direct view. Because of this, their ears are designed to collect sounds from the widest possible angle. The ears of most birds are small round holes, but owls have thin, crescent-shaped slits behind each eye that can take up almost the whole side of the skull in some species. The greater size of the ears reflects their importance. Not only do owls' ears warn them of approaching danger, they help them catch prey.

Ear position

The strangest aspect of some owls' ears is that, in strictly nocturnal species such as **tawnies**, **long-eared** and **wood owls**, they are neither identical nor positioned symmetrically. Normally the right ear is larger than the left by as much as 50 per cent. It is also usually higher on the owl's head than the left ear. In some species, such as **Tengmalm's**, the ears are so different that the shape of the skull itself has changed. The slight bulge that accommodates the ears is high up on the right side and low down on the left, giving the bird's head a strange, lopsided appearance. This peculiar arrangement helps the owl accurately analyse even the smallest rustles of undergrowth. Sound location with two ears is worked out by directly comparing the signals picked up by each ear. Obviously, the ear closer to the source will be the first to detect any sound, even though it may only do so 1/300,000th of a second before the other.

Our own ears are a matched pair in size and position, so we can identify the approximate direction of a sound but not much else. Because the ears of an owl are not identical, they each pick up a slightly different sound and this extra information allows a far more detailed picture to be constructed. The two 'sound-fixes' help the owl to construct a three-dimensional image in exactly the same way as stereoscopic vision does. This is particularly useful when trying to locate a moving object. Identical ears have great difficulty

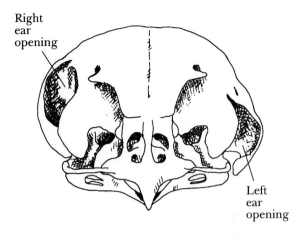

Right ear opening

Left ear opening

The Tengmalm's owl's skull is lopsided because it has to accommodate the asymmetric ears characteristic of nocturnal owls

pinpointing movement, as each one picks up the same sound. But in an asymmetrical system any change, such as the increase or decrease in the level of noise as the animal runs around, is different in each ear. This gives the owl enough information to fix the prey precisely, even while it is moving.

When an owl hears a disturbance, it weaves its head to and fro in the general direction of the noise. Because of the design of the unmatched sound system, when the bird hears a noise with the same intensity in each ear, then it is looking directly at the animal making it. The owl does not have to think, it merely has to move its head until the signals match in each ear.

Long-eared owl

Ear flaps

To help home in on small sounds, owls have a curious mechanism that acts in the same way as the ears of a mouse. Nocturnal mammals have dish-shaped hearing receivers that can swivel about and be 'aimed' at an interesting sound. These channel the soundwaves into the inner ear, helping to make the hearing more selective. Although owls do not have true external ears, they do use flaps of skin and short stubby feathers just in front and behind their ear-openings. These flaps are known as *opercula* and they can be moved at will. A sleeping owl will have the earflaps closed down, but a wary or hungry owl will raise them and the effect is probably similar to a human cupping his hand behind or in front of his ear to detect dim and distant sounds. This 'focusing' of their ears helps owls to fix a sound source to within an angle of just one degree, a feat that is well beyond our own ability.

There is one more sophisticated physical advantage that owls have over man and that is the mechanism that relays soundwaves from the eardrum to the inner ear. We have three small bones (ossicles) that connect the two and amplify the sound about twenty times; owls have a single, complex bone known as the *stapes*, which amplifies sound sixty-five times. Soft sounds that are lost in our ear mechanism would therefore be detected by the owl's keen hearing.

The effectiveness of an owl's hearing changes, however, as frequency fluctuates. It has now been disovered that owls are hopeless at pinpointing the source of low-frequency sounds. If the bird hears a noise with a frequency below 5 kilohertz, it seems to be completely baffled about its exact origin even though it is aware that something is happening. As the pitch gets higher, the owl's ability to locate the sound increases. This is because the angle of their ears' sensitivity decreases as the frequency rises. Owls can detect low-pitched sounds from all around, but higher sounds can only be picked up in a narrow angle immediately in front of the bird's head. This is a great advantage to predators that hunt rodents – animals that use high frequency for communication. It is no coincidence that owls have evolved hearing that is finely 'tuned-in' to the same wavelength as their prey.

As the ears pick up different 'bits' of sound information, not only can the owl work out the direction of its prey, but also exactly how far away it is. By comparing the angles of maximum 'loudness' in both ears, a hunting owl gets two distinct bearings and the unsuspecting prey waits where the imaginary lines bisect. These specialised abilities would be of little use unless the owl can interpret the complex information, so the hearing centre of an owl's brain is much larger than in diurnal birds of a similar size. (The barn owl has 97,000 neurons in its auditory centre while the crow, twice the size, has only 27,000).

Hunting in darkness

Detailed and meticulous experiments have shown that some species, such as the **barn owl** and **long-eared owl,** can hunt successfully in absolute, scientific darkness, simply by using their hearing alone. Early experimenters tried putting out dead mice for captive owls and, at each session, steadily reduced the light levels until the time arrived when the bird could not find the food. They then announced that owls could hunt in light conditions down to a specific measured level. But this ignored the fact that owls are not carrion eaters and only rarely eat prey that is already dead. Inside a laboratory they may have been unable to see a dead mouse in darkness, but in the real world they hunt for animals that move and scratch and squeak.

A far more elegant experiment took place in complete darkness using a barn owl. The laboratory was carpeted with twigs, leaves and other undergrowth, and the owl was given plenty of time to get to know the layout of the room before the test began. When a live mouse was released, the owl reacted as soon as the rodent started to move through the leaf litter. Within seconds the mouse was dead, located and caught in absolute darkness by a barn owl listening to the sounds of a tiny animal moving through the leaves.

It was later realised that the owl actually needed at least two 'sound-guides'. The first was to alert it to the presence of prey, which would trigger the take-off and dictate the direction. The owl then needed another sound, while in flight, to pinpoint exactly where the mouse was. If there was only one sound, the catch-rate dropped dramatically, which is one reason why small, nocturnal animals freeze all movement when they suspect that an enemy is close. If it makes no noise, a mouse is much less likely to be caught by an owl. This method of listening to prey while flying also helps to explain just why owls have evolved silent flight. The noise made by conventional feathers would mask the rustle of a mouse as it scuttled through the undergrowth.

In reality, even if the condition existed, no owl would choose to hunt in absolute darkness; they may have the physical ability to catch prey successfully, but they would run the risk of flying into large, soundless objects such as trees. The majority of truly nocturnal species stay in one area and never venture far; it is in their interest to learn where the obstacles are, so that they can be avoided. But even owls are not infallible. This was proved when the experiment entered the next stage. Pieces of paper were tied to lengths of string and pulled through the leaves in jerks that sounded just like a hesitant mouse. The owl would strike within seconds of hearing the paper rustle. But, in the darkness, it completely ignored the soundless run of a live mouse crossing a hard concrete floor.

I was once introduced to an old, female tawny owl that had been in captivity for more than five years. She had been found lying on a lawn beneath a low overhead cable. She must have been out on a hunting flight, five metres above the ground, carefully scrutinising the grass below. While concentrating on the search for prey, she did not notice the thin strands of the telegraph wire a few inches in front of her and smashed into them.

Despite a great deal of care and attention, the tawny lost the sight of both eyes, but was otherwise fit and healthy. The only sign of injury was a faint milky colour in both eyes. She settled down to life in the rescue centre, but feeding was a real problem. She couldn't see her food and, because the mice were dead, she couldn't hear them move. Very few people are willing to feed live animals to captive birds as it is cruel and is of absolutely no benefit to the bird. So this tawny was fed on a piece of newspaper, to amplify the sound, with dead mice that were dragged noisily on a length of string because this was the only way that she could locate them. She got the idea within two days and from then on the feeding equipment consisted of three mice, a newspaper and a ball of string. It worked every time!

In their natural habitat, owls do not exist in a world of total blackness. To catch their prey they use a combination of sight and hearing, depending upon the time, prey and weather conditions, amongst other things. And there are considerable differences between species. It is thought that owls with large eyes rely pri-

This barn owl has just caught a bank vole

marily on eyesight, with hearing a complementary sense. The **European eagle owl** has huge eyes, but its ears show little asymmetry, which would make precise sound-location difficult. These enormous birds can take very large prey and have little need to listen for small rustlings.

The **great grey owl** is a very large bird, but its eyes are tiny in comparison. However, its ears show the classic owl design, one large and the other small. Great greys feed mainly on voles, wary creatures that stay beneath the safety of grass and are very difficult to find. Without acute hearing, the great greys would go hungry.

Speaking generally, it is the more **nocturnal species** that have the most sensitive hearing, while the others rely mainly on sight.

One recent theory is that the further away a species lives from the equator, the better its hearing is likely to be. Countless species of animals are found in the tropics and many are nocturnal. The incessant call of cicadas, tree frogs and other creatures would thoroughly confuse a hunting owl that relied completely on sound-location. Northern forests and farmland are much quieter places. Here, there is little to interfere with the owl's extraordinary sense of hearing.

European eagle owl with 'ear' tufts relaxed

4 The Silent Hunter

Every year I give dozens of talks on owls to an assortment of groups ranging from infant schools to conservation groups and every kind of society in between. While I should know better by now, I am always surprised by the preconceptions many people have about these birds, and in particular, about the owl's diet. Whenever I take a live owl to a talk there is a strong chance that someone will inquire whether it will eat peanuts or popcorn, bread or biscuits – whatever snack is available. The answer is no to all of them. Owls are purely **carnivorous**, they only ever eat meat.

Where owls are concerned, 'meat' can mean any animal from the size of an earthworm upwards. The size of prey depends upon the species, although most owls are non-specialised hunters and will eat almost anything they can catch. The idea of strong, quick animals killing and eating smaller ones frequently causes concern to non-naturalists, but they are only making a human's emotional response and applying it to an animal's instinctive and unalterable behaviour. Owls kill and eat other creatures simply because it is the only way to survive. Unlike some humans, they do not kill for pleasure or out of anger, but to feed themselves and their young, and occasionally to protect their nests. Owls never catch more than they need to eat as that would be a waste of valuable energy. They have to kill because they are anatomically designed to eat only meat and cannot digest any other type of food.

In every habitat, the high mortality rate of smaller animals due to owls and other predators influences the smaller creatures' reproductive rates. Rats, mice, rabbits and other small animals all produce far more young than are needed to keep their numbers healthy. The food chain has evolved over generations and a fine balance between all of the species must be maintained if the system is to work correctly. Without prey, the predators would die out. Without the controlling effects of carnivores, there would be a population explosion of prey species and they would run out of space and food.

Nocturnal mammals, like this wood mouse, have very sensitive ears that can pick up the slightest sound

Beaks

Owls are perfectly equipped to catch prey, but even their 'weapons' are often misunderstood. Although the **hooked beaks** look sharp and powerful, they are not the most dangerous part of an owl's armoury and can do little damage; they certainly cannot 'bite your finger off'. The muscles controlling the beak are surprisingly weak and, like all other birds, owls do not have teeth. The beak is more of a tool than anything else, to be used for tearing off small pieces of meat, and only if all else fails will owls use them to kill small animals such as mice.

Talons

It is the lethally powerful, sharp talons that deliver the *coup de grâce* which actually kills the chosen prey and, from far too many past experiences, I can report that they are infinitely stronger than they appear.

The legs of most owls are designed in the same way – they are muscular and long, although much of their length is hidden by the chest feathers. The vast majority of owls have short, thin feathers, which look more like hairs, all the way down to their toes. These are densely packed to give some protection from the teeth of prey which might try to fight back by biting the owl's legs. The 'leggings' also help keep the birds warm during cold nights, when they sit waiting for prey.

The feet of birds of prey have to be stronger and more versatile than those of other species because they have to perch, walk and kill equally well. There is a universal foot design for perching birds that consists of four toes, three facing forward and one back (like the human thumb) so that they can both grip on to branches and balance on the ground. Owls' feet follow the same basic pattern but also feature a novel modification. The outside toe on each foot is reversible; it can face either forwards or backwards. At rest it lies in the conventional position or slightly out to the side. Only when the owl comes in for the kill does the outside toe swing around 180º, just before the strike. The arrangement of two toes in front and two behind evenly distributes the bird's strength, giving a grip that often kills within seconds. If the impact and squeeze does not kill, prey will be quickly finished off with a swift bite to the back of the neck.

The smaller species have a mechanism that locks their talons into a tight grip for a short time after the strike to keep the pressure applied and help prevent the prey from escaping. I remember once being presented with an injured barn owl that had been rescued from the embrace of an unfriendly cat. When I picked up the bird to take a closer look, the lady rescuer pointed to a spot on the owl's chest where she had seen some blood. She showed a dangerous disregard for the bird's feet, and the owl had an equal scorn for its benefactor. Faster than the eye could follow, and before I could warn her, a talon wrapped around the fleshy part of her thumb.

If any other species has sharper claws than a barn owl, I have yet to meet it. Their claws are like finely honed needles. Not only do they grip with surprising power, but they all curl inwards simultaneously. The result is like being attacked by four fishing hooks. It does not need much imagination to work out what would happen to a mouse under the same conditions. As soon as I carefully removed one talon from the lady rescuer's thumb and went to work on the next, the first one locked itself back into the killing grip. Unlatching the squeezing talons of a determined owl is always a tricky and painful operation. The good samaritan suffered in silence and after a few painful minutes I managed to prise the owl away from its victim. A small animal that found itself in this situation would not have been so fortunate.

Hunting from a perch

Before attempting a kill, the owl has to find suitable prey, and it has two rough strategies. The most common technique is to sit on a convenient perch and wait until an animal of the right size passes by. The owl watches from a high point, like a branch or telegraph pole, and quietly surveys the ground beneath. It is now that the ball-and-socket action of the owl's head comes in useful. Nocturnal animals have keen hearing and the small ones are constantly alert for the slightest noise that announces the presence of a big animal. If the owl had to turn around to search for prey behind, the sound of talons scraping on a branch would give out a warning signal that something large and dangerous was nearby. Using their highly mobile necks, owls can look all around without once having to move.

When prey is spotted, it is just a short swoop down to the next meal. The owl pounces with head back and legs stretched out towards the target, which means that the weapons strike first while the most vulnerable part of the bird, its head, is kept as far away as possible in case the selected prey makes a fight of it. For the same reason, most owls

The talons of an eagle owl are not sharp, they rely on pure strength to kill prey

close their eyes a split-second before impact to protect their sight. This wait-and-see method is very economical in terms of energy, but it does need a perch that is very close to a rich hunting ground. During a single night, a hungry owl might use many tried and tested perches until it has eaten enough.

When catching prey, owls strike with talons outstretched and head back

Hunting from the air

The other main hunting technique involves looking for prey from the air. **Barn owls** are probably the most expert at hunting on the wing. They slowly float low over fields, occasionally dipping down into the grass after a mouse; their light body weight and large wings make flight easy work and they can cover a lot of ground in a short time. It is always better, however, to look for a moving subject from a still position. The task is made more difficult when the viewer is also in motion. Under the right conditions an owl will hover for a short time, keeping its head stationary relative to the ground while watching for movements below. **Hawk owls** are particularly good at this approach, but they cannot keep it up for long, unlike kestrels and hummingbirds, which are the true masters of hovering skills. Hawk owls are very un-owl-like creatures; with their sleek bodies and long tails they really do resemble hawks. In their arctic and subarctic homelands, they sit on exposed perches such as the point of a low tree and watch for small mammals. With a very swift dart and short hover, the hawk owl quickly makes a catch and returns to its observation point.

Hunting on foot

There are some species that actually hunt on foot. The tiny **burrowing owl** from the Americas will frequently sprint along the ground when chasing the invertebrates that make up 90 per cent of its diet. They can produce short bursts of surprising speed and their long legs are well suited to life in grazed grassland.

As their name suggests, these owls nest in underground burrows. They are quite capable of excavating their own tunnels but more often they will move into second-hand homes that have been abandoned by armadillos or skunks. Recently they have taken up residence in man-made habitats and can be found living on airfields and golf courses. One burrowing owl tunnel, on the edge of a course in Texas, was found to have twenty-seven used balls close to the underground nest. These owls are much too small to carry golf balls and it is a mystery how so many ended up in this particular spot.

Airfields can be excellent sites for owl spotting. While sitting in a plane that was slowly getting into position for take-off at Toronto International, I once watched a lone snowy owl sitting on a signpost in the centre of the maze of runways. It was dwarfed – and undaunted – by the non-stop activity of colossal screaming jets that surrounded it. During the two or three minutes that I watched through the tiny window, the snowy did not move, and I imagine it was deeply engrossed in the age-old owl occupation of waiting for prey. It reminded me of the snowy owls that overwinter at Kennedy Airport, New York, and feed on mainly black-tailed jack rabbits, introduced animals whose ancestors escaped

Owls catch prey with their sharp talons and death is instantaneous

from a live shipment that was passing through. They found the grassy areas of the international airport to their liking and now breed freely.

Owls have a **high metabolic rate** and their body temperature is 5° C higher than our own. A system like this needs a lot of fuel, but unlike carnivorous mammals, owls only ever eat enough food to replace the energy that has been used since their last meal. Once that level has been reached, they simply return to a safe roost to sleep and preen.

Owls all have an optimum body weight at which they function most effectively; over-eating and the storage of excess food as extra fat would mean that their weight would become too high for flight and this could be fatal. They are physically unable to eat more than they immediately need. Unlike the day-time birds of prey, owls do not have crops. These are expanding pouches in the gullet where a large amount of food can be stored before digestion. They have to eat small quantities at regular intervals. In lean times, when food is difficult to find, owls often become too weak to hunt. Powered flight burns up a great deal of energy; the more a bird flies, the more it must eat and yet in order to catch food an owl must fly. It is a carefully balanced equation that can easily be disturbed. When owls become too weak to fly, they will stay on the ground and hunt for less energetic prey. Most will take earthworms, beetles and a wide range of insects when they are truly hungry. However, there is not as much energy-giving food in invertebrates as there is in an equal weight of small mammals, so it takes some time to rebuild their energy levels this way.

During a single night an 'average' **tawny owl** is supposed to eat **eight mouse-size animals.** A more realistic list is likely to include frogs, dragonflies, moths, beetles and even bats. The list changes with the seasons. Winter months, with their characteristic low undergrowth, are good for catching rodents as there is little in the way of ground cover to hide them. In spring, once the plants have reappeared, more insects are taken. Young, inexperienced owls that have only just left the nest often have problems adapting to catching their own food. For the first few weeks their diet can consist entirely of earthworms,

Owls share remarkably stricking facial similarities with other birds of prey - like this buzzard for instance

which are less awkward to catch than mice.

Despite the owl's formidable senses and physical advantages, it is not always successful at hunting. The eyes and ears of prey animals are just as well developed as the owl's and all small animals regularly stop to look around, listen and scent the air for signs of danger. With eyes on the sides of their head, mice have a wide angle of vision and their nocturnal sight is very good. Their ears often act like radar dishes and can hear the slightest sound. Often they detect an approaching enemy and

escape well before it is within striking distance.

Killing prey

Small owls rely mainly on their strong squeeze to dispose of prey. Bigger ones, however, have the added advantage of weight. **Eagle owls** can weigh up to four kilogrammes. When dropping on to prey at 40 kilometres an hour, the initial impact causes a lot of damage, even before the talons are used. It must be similar to a heavy shopping bag being dropped onto a human's head from a second-storey window. Such an aerial attack, when used with a grip that is far stronger than that of a fully grown man, makes this species one of the world's most powerful birds. Because of their high energy requirements, eagle owls concentrate on hunting mammals, which give plenty of food for the expended effort, and they can catch anything up to the size of a young roe deer. But they are not fussy eaters, and have been known to hunt domestic cats, dogs, foxes and even hedgehogs – they probably have the most wide-ranging diet of any bird of prey.

Whenever a small owl kills, it either swallows the food immediately or takes it to the relative safety of a high perch. This is not to prevent the food from being stolen, but for self-preservation. During eating, an owl's guard is down and it could be pounced upon

European eagle owl with rabbit

and eaten by a passing fox. The bigger species are a little more confident and will normally eat on the ground – few foxes would have the nerve to try to steal a meal from an eagle owl.

Owls are certainly not the soft cuddly creatures they first seem. They will kill anything smaller than themselves and that includes other owls. The angelic-looking, wide-eyed **tawny owl** is a major predator of the **scops owl** in southern Europe. But it doesn't have things all its own way, as **eagle owls** are known to eat tawny owls. The list goes on: **great horned owls** will kill **screech owls** and almost all of them will eat the young of other species, given the chance.

Eating prey

Once the prey is caught, the owl must then eat it. Small animals are swallowed whole (owls cannot chew) but bigger ones need to be handled differently. When eating a rabbit, an eagle owl will hold it down with one foot and pull pieces off with the beak. Manageable portions are not surgically cut off, they are pulled away using the strong neck muscles. The beak is just a hook for gripping. We can tear newspapers in half even though we do not have sharp hands; it is all done with muscle power.

If the owl is really hungry, all the rabbit will be eaten. Owls need not only to eat the meat but also the bones and fur. First-time owl keepers, trying to be kind, regularly feed

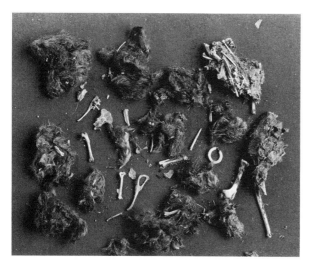

Dissected pellet of a short-eared owl showing the remains of several field voles

their animals on high quality dressed meat from a butcher. For a while the bird will do well, but slowly it will weaken and become more susceptible to disease and infection. Meat alone does not provide enough of the owl's dietary needs. It must have roughage, vitamins, minerals and trace elements that are found in other parts of the animal's body such as the bones and fur.

Pellets

An owl's stomach cannot dissolve and absorb all the hard parts of such a meal; in fact its digestive juices are not as strong as those of diurnal birds of prey and much remains undigested. Skulls, teeth, fur, feathers and other tough substances are compressed into a **sausage-shaped pellet** while inside the owl and are regurgitated twice a day. The process of bringing up a pellet looks very uncomfortable – to force it up and out, the muscles have to reverse the normal downwards action of swallowing, and it can take some time to expel a large pellet.

There is nothing nasty or unpleasant about pellets. When they first emerge they are a little slimy due to the thin coating of mucus which lubricates them during regurgitation, but they soon dry into hard, lightweight cylinders. Fortunately for the naturalist, many owls are creatures of habit and usually drop pellets in the same place each day. Good daytime roosts of barn owls might be used by successive generations and old roosts are constantly being found where pellets, dating back many years, lie several inches deep.

A pile of owl pellets is a mine of information to an expert with the skill to interpret the signs. Under a microscope and with a good reference book, the species of each skull, tooth and vertebra can be exactly identified. The contents can even show when times are bad and the owl has been forced to catch insects, for even the thin wing-cases of beetles can be seen.

Pellet analysis is an ideal way of studying the long-term food source of owls and this is one of the best-understood areas of their biology. It shows how the diet alters in different habitats even within the same species. Pellets also confirm the fact that owls are opportunistic feeders and will take whatever is available. For instance, a large proportion of a **rural tawny owl's** diet is made up of rodents, with small birds only occupying a minor part; **urban tawnies**, on the other hand, prey mainly on roosting birds because most of the wild mice live indoors and few other small animals can be found.

Pellet enthusiasts often find that, if they leave dried pellets around for too long, they attract the attention of other interested parties, such as moths. Before man appeared on the scene and considerately produced an endless quantity of blankets and pullovers, dried owl pellets would have been one of the original breeding grounds for several species of clothes moths. The clean, dried and undigested fur and feathers in a pellet are perfect for a female moth looking for a substance that will provide food for her hungry larvae when they first hatch from the tiny eggs.

One interesting discovery made from pellets is that individual owls have tastes of their own, even within identical habitats. While all birds of one species will eat the same range of prey animals, most individuals show a distinct preference for a particular food. This is not the same as a human's food fad, because owls do not chew and savour every morsel. It is not brought about by enjoyment of a specific flavour, but more as the result of personal experience. Young owls are not born with hunting skills, they have to learn the intricacies and science of catching prey. Early

attempts are usually disastrous, with the owl crashing into the undergrowth and completely missing its target. With practice the owl becomes more proficient, and it does learn from its mistakes, but the first prey that is successfully taken during this critical learning period will probably be a favourite choice for the rest of the bird's life.

This can cause difficulties when young owls come into contact with humans for any length of time. I was once presented with a little owl by the local police. From the look of its fluffy feathers the bird had not been out of the nest for long, but in that short time it had managed to have, and lose, an argument with a car. The injuries were not bad but the owl had to stay with us for ten days to recuperate and fill up on a diet of dead mice.

Contact with injured, and particularly young, owls is always kept to a bare minimum for the sake of the patient's state of mind and to keep it 'wild'. Since this owl was too young to have established a territory of its own, we released it into our garden. It takes time for an injured bird to get back into the habit of being wild and hunting for itself, so for the first few days of freedom we often leave out food while the bird resharpens its skills. Every evening at about six o'clock, I dropped two dead mice on to a high brick wall at the end of the garden; ten seconds later the owl would silently swoop down to eat.

After four days the bird sat in an ash tree close to the wall, as if waiting for me. It showed no fear but would not let me come closer than a metre or so. By the end of the week the little owl had become a permanent and obvious resident in the garden. Its favourite daytime perch was a shady stretch of washing line, that passed just beneath an ancient, drooping apple tree. We knew exactly where it was but, although postmen and milkmen went by daily within a few steps of it, they did not notice its presence. If ever I was late bringing food, the impatient owl sat on the roof of my studio and shrieked loudly. Little owls always look as if they are frowning at the best of times, and when calling for supper this one would stretch up to its full majestic height of 25 centimetres and give out short yelps that could be heard by half the village.

It reached the stage when the owl relied totally on me for food; it seldom left the garden and spent its life sitting and preening – the owl equivalent of a couch-potato. I didn't begrudge buying the food, but I certainly did not want to encourage bad habits amongst local owls. It was a painful decision but finally I cut the owl's rations by half. The bird's opinion was only too obvious – it stood on the roof and shrieked its displeasure, demanding its fair share of mice. The poor starving bird didn't have to go far for food as our garden has been carefully designed and nurtured as a haven for wildlife. Amongst the log piles, long grass and nettles there are dozens of wood mice, field voles and countless worms and beetles. The little owl did not even have

to leave the security of the garden to feed. But this one had become lazy and had learned that it was easier to eat an already dead, fast-food mouse than actually to go out to look and kill for itself.

The following week was noisy and uncomfortable; the little owl did not allow itself to be weaned on to natural food without a fight. Each night, after eating the token offering I had left out, it stood on the studio roof and declared its hunger to the world before going off in search of food the old-fashioned way. Within a week it had become a rare visitor and, judging by its rotund appearance, the learning process may have been traumatic but it had also been successful.

It is not only ornithologists who closely monitor pellets. Mammal biologists can winkle out just as much, but very different, data from detailed analysis. It is safe to assume that, within any given habitat, owls' feeding behaviour does not change greatly from year to year – their diet should remain much the same with only slight variations. If the contents of the pellets alter, this quickly shows up fluctuations in the populations of the animals they are eating. The accuracy of this technique has been cross-checked, using several other methods to test the results, and it is one of the most precise ways of monitoring levels of prey species.

The bodies of all animals, particularly birds and mammals, contain a high percentage of water. It is stored in the meat, internal organs

This little owl would not leave our garden after being fed by humans for only a short time

and blood, all of which are absorbed by the owl as it eats its prey. Because owls have a thick layer of feathers they do not sweat and, although they lose water through breathing, their moisture loss is very low. As a result, owls rarely drink as they get most of the water they need from their prey.

Winter feeding

In cold weather, food consumption needs to be dramatically increased to maintain their high body temperature. Unfortunately this coincides with a seasonal drop in the number of prey animals. There are no large insects about, earthworms are deep beneath the soil and few small mammals give birth during the winter months. Predators are forced to compete for an ever-dwindling food supply at a time when they need more than ever. The highest number of owl deaths comes at the very end of winter, when the mammal population has been cut drastically by the combination of cold, hunger and predation and their numbers have not been replenished by the production of young. By this time the owl's body weight can be getting dangerously low and hunting becomes more difficult. In the winter it is possible to see some owls hunting in daylight, as they cannot always find enough food at night.

Winter also brings the added complication of snow. After a heavy fall, when the fields are covered in a deep blanket of white, a vital part of the owl's food almost disappears.

Small mammals, such as mice and voles, actually stay beneath the snow. Their own food, seeds and grass left from the previous autumn, is at ground level. Above the snow there is nothing to eat and they are completely exposed; underneath they can feed and are safe from attack.

In these conditions, owls have to rely entirely on their hearing in order to eat. The faint sound made by a moving mouse, muffled by snow, is the only clue to the presence of food. They have to crash through the snow layer to reach their prey below. The **great grey owl**, from the northern reaches of Europe and Canada, is a master of this technique. Its relatively small eyes point to the fact that hearing is the prime sense and research has shown that they have huge ear openings and possess one of the best sound-gathering systems of all living birds. Great greys are imposing beasts and look like one of the largest of all owls. But their appearance is deceiving, as more than half of their bulk is made up of thick, soft feathers that insulate them against the biting cold. The owl's body is much smaller than it looks.

Voles are common in the subarctic and the great grey has become something of an expert in catching them. However, living so far north, they have to hunt in snowfields that do not melt for many months. Much of the

European eagle owls generally avoid dense woodland, preferring more open ground

procedure is uneventful and quiet – the owl sits motionless on a perch, first fixing its head towards one patch of snow for a minute or so and then swivelling around to face the other way. It can be so absorbed in listening that it ignores the approach of a careful, quiet human. Then, without warning, signalled by a movement audible only to the owl, it takes off and crashes through the snow at high speed. Great greys have been known to take voles that are 45 centimetres beneath the surface and, in the process, almost disappear under the snow themselves. Most owls can do this to some extent in a shallow blanket of soft, newly fallen snow; but after a freeze, when it is compacted and coated with ice, the mice are well protected from the less specialised species.

When the ground is covered in snow, and only then, will owls take carrion. Many species are known to eat fish lying dead on the bank of a river, and some have been known to take animals from traps. Keen owl-watchers can even coax their hungry subjects to come down to a bird table in cold weather. The ideal bait is dead mice, but they are not always available. With a little perseverance and luck, wild owls can be persuaded to eat cat food left on a high wall or garden shed. A word of warning, though: try to make the bait inaccessible if you don't want to attract the neighbourhood cats as well.

Appalling weather is a universal enemy of all wildlife and in the wake of a cold snap there will be the remains of small birds and animals around that have not survived. While their thin bodies offer little food to a hungry owl, these scraps are better than nothing. **Snowy owls**, for instance, live in a hostile environment that suffers terrible wind and cold during much of the year. These birds have to take food whenever the opportunity arises and will feed off any dead animal they can find. Snowies are one of the few owls that build up a layer of body fat when there is a surplus of food available, which acts as a reserve to be used when times are harder. Eskimos kill snowy owls in order to eat the rich store of fat, but hunting these wary birds takes skill and the Eskimos only catch a relatively small number in a year. Apparently, although I personally have not tried it and am sure I never will, owl flesh is stringy and not at all good to eat.

Hunting can be difficult and unpredictable for just a single owl, but it is even more demanding and time-consuming when there is the added responsibility of young to feed.

5 Family Life

Birds that eat insects or seeds do not often have to compete with each other for food as, for most of the year, there is usually enough to go round. In fact, it can be a great advantage to stay together and feed in a large flock because each individual has a much better chance of survival if a predator attacks. An owl's food, however, is less plentiful and more difficult to collect. Direct competition makes the task even more complicated, so each bird energetically defends its hunting territory against any rival that attempts to move in. This aggressive behaviour ensures that owls are solitary creatures which spend much of the year alone. There are one or two species, however, that do come together in groups. **Long-eared owls** have community roosts in winter and up to fifty birds have been known to perch in a single clump of trees. But at dusk they go hunting alone, and the common roost is merely a convenience.

I remember walking through a field of very long grass on a bitterly cold February day when a short-eared owl rose just a few metres in front of me, disturbed by my loud footsteps. Within seconds nine more appeared from the same part of the field and, for a short time, the sky seemed to be filled with these long-winged birds. The owls quickly vanished, each going in a different direction but, judging from their take-off point, they must have been sitting very close together.

In owl circles, possession is 90 per cent of the law and this tenet dictates their attitudes to other owls. In Sweden the **ural owl** is called *slaguggla* – the attacking owl – because it will violently chase and even kill tawny owls that attempt to nest within the boundaries of its territory. Resident owls have the 'moral upper ground', and will forcibly drive away intruders of either sex as soon as they are detected.

Enforced protection of a hunting territory is an excellent policy, as it keeps the food supply private and safe. During the breeding season, though, this antisocial behaviour is potentially a major problem. Although the male is more aggressive, the female is

European eagle owl – threat display

stronger, so both animals need to show restraint to form a successful bond.

Nesting territories

The staking of a nesting territory begins in autumn. Male tawny owls are very vocal at this time of year, proclaiming ownership with loud, penetrating calls. This will be the first indication to local females that a male is close and has found a good nest-site. From then on he will roost close to his selected nest and defend the area against all comers in preparation for the breeding season.

Nocturnal owls, such as tawnies, advertise for mates by using their calls; but when trying to attract females, the males of **diurnal** species make the most of the available daylight by giving ostentatious flying displays. Both **snowy** and **short-eared owls,** for instance, fly high and elaborately over the nest-site. The short-eareds have a wide-ranging circular courtship flight where they exaggerate their normal action, clapping their wings together on the down beat so that they can be seen and heard at the same time.

In spring it is usually the female that moves into the male's territory. For most of the year this act would bring swift and violent retaliation and she needs to be very submissive during the first stages of courtship if she is to avoid being attacked. For a while the two birds will sit in nearby trees and call to each other as a sign of recognition and to start breaking down the natural hostility. Slowly

A short-eared owl giving a threat display

they move closer. The male will offer food to his mate – this is a good move as it shows that his intentions are not aggressive, helps to calm her, and proves that he is a good provider. All of these preliminaries take place very near to the probable nest-site and fix the spot in the minds of both partners.

The first physical contact comes when they preen each other. This is not to clean feathers, but is more of a ritual to ease tension. Many owls rub beaks with their partner and actually seem to enjoy each other's company. They sleep close together and by this stage the relationship is cemented.

This attentive behaviour continues throughout the breeding season to help maintain and strengthen the pair-bond; the two may be nesting and rearing young, but the innate rivalry is never far beneath the surface and must be tightly controlled for the benefit of both. As well as keeping the breeding relationship in working order and supplying food, the male constantly has to defend the site against the attentions of unpaired males trying to seduce his female.

Mating can only take place when the female is completely receptive and at ease, since the male must perch on his mate's back, which requires the co-operation of both birds. Should he make his move too early, the action could be misinterpreted, the female might feel she had to defend herself and could possibly kill him. To communicate her readiness to mate, the female uses a series of soft calls that tell her partner that all is safe.

Making a nest
Small birds build an amazing variety of nests. Weaver birds, bower birds and numerous others skilfully produce breeding dens of astonishing complexity. Owls, however, **lack even the most basic nest-building talent**. Their eggs are white and the total absence of camouflage suggests that owls originally evolved as a group of hole-nesters. Eggs in more exposed nests are cryptically coloured with random patches of brown or blue to break up their outline and make them more difficult to spot from above. Camouflage is not an important consideration for a nest tucked away safely inside a hollow tree; and white eggs are easier to find in darkness – even for an owl. Another pointer to the hole theory is that owl eggs are more rounded than those of other birds. Conventional 'egg-shaped' eggs will not roll far if disturbed, they just go around in a small circle. This prevents them from falling from a ledge or out of a flat nest – a problem that doesn't arise inside a hole.

The majority of the world's owls are hole-nesters. Most choose hollow trees, others move into abandoned buildings or man-made nest boxes. The tiny **elf owl**, from southern parts of the USA and Mexico, lays its eggs in cavities originally excavated by Gila woodpeckers. There are few trees in this dry, semi-desert environment, so the owls and woodpeckers nest inside a giant Saguaro cactus. The final result is the same: the holes in both trees and cacti are warm, dry and safe from most predators.

The owls that have abandoned holes are those that have moved away from mature deciduous woodlands, the habitat in which they probably evolved. **Short-eared owls** are masters of open moorland, where they search for field voles on the ground amongst the heather and bracken. They also nest on the ground. The clutch of four to eight eggs is laid in a rough hollow in the shelter of tall grass or heather.

In the barren northern tundra surrounding the Arctic Circle, where there are no trees at all, the **snowy owl's** nest can be completely exposed. The 'scrape' is often on a ridge or hummock to give the birds a good all-round view, making a surprise attack from predators very unlikely.

Barn owls in a nest box

Long-eared owls are primarily birds of coniferous forests. Fir trees, however, do not rot and split in the same way as broadleaved trees and usually fall to the ground before their middle rots, making large holes scarce. Even under these trying conditions, long-eareds do not attempt to build nests of their own. They commandeer old ones made the previous year by crows, pigeons or even squirrels. They do, however, at least make an attempt to improve the site, and have been seen adding twigs to an existing nest to make

Barn owl chicks in captivity

it into the cup-shape that they prefer. Just occasionally, they will nest on the ground. This laid-back approach is far from unique, for **great greys**, **great horned**, **fish owls**, **ural owls** and several others regularly take the option of 'squatting' rather than making their own nests.

A good nest-site, protected against the elements and close to rich hunting grounds, will be used every year by successive generations. Most species of owls usually pair for life while both partners are alive, but this does not often last long, mainly because it is unlikely that both will survive for more than two or three seasons.

Owls mate with their nearest available partner and if neither moves away then they will still be neighbours when the next breeding season starts. When either disappears, however, its place will be taken by another convenient bird. The bigger species, such as **great horned**, **eagle owl** and **snowy**, have long life spans and will often pair with the same mate for several successive seasons.

They are generally monogamous birds, male owls mating with just one female at a time, although there are exceptions. Feeding chicks, however, can be an exhausting task and, unless there is a real plague of prey animals to be taken, supplying food to two different nests would be impossible.

In the spring, the male and female come together for a specific task – to raise young. Once the young have flown, the adults have no real contact with each other. They will probably stay in the same area but should they accidentally meet again, before the pairing time, they will treat each other as rivals for food.

Incubation

Most species of owls lay their eggs at two-day intervals until the clutch is complete and incubation begins with the first egg. The **pygmy owl** is unusual as it waits for the arrival of the last egg before sitting. These birds are the size of chunky sparrows and have one more unusual nesting ploy. To tempt the female into the chosen nest for the first time, the male will leave an item of highly prized prey, such as a song thrush or redwing, inside the hole.

The size of all owls' clutches is controlled by the availability of food. In good years the number of eggs can be 50 per cent higher than average. When hunting is poor the owls may not nest at all, but this happens only rarely. While the relationship between predators and prey seems to be heavily in favour of the hunters, the balance is not as one-sided as a casual viewer might first think. It is true that the hunting activities of the predators do have a controlling influence on the population of the prey. It is equally true that, as the breeding potential of predators is linked to the food supply, the prey exerts a similar regulation on the number of owls that eat them.

As a rule, big, strong animals have fewer

young because their size – and protection by even more powerful parents – makes them less likely to be eaten by other animals, so the percentage mortality rate is lower. It also takes longer for them to reach independence, so they eat more food and each chick is a considerable drain on the adults' resources. This is reflected in the size of clutches. **Eagle owls** produce two or three eggs while the much smaller **hawk owl** has been known to lay twelve. The difference in the survival rate levels the numbers out. The smaller owls might have more chicks, but only a few survive to breeding age, so the population growth is similar to that of the bigger species.

The job of incubating the eggs belongs exclusively to the female in all but a few species. At the beginning of incubation, a 'brood patch' appears on her underside. The skin loses its feathers and the veins beneath become enlarged to give off extra heat. This bald, warm patch is laid directly on to the eggs while the female is sitting. Her higher body weight and greater food reserves mean that she is better suited than the male to endure the energy-sapping rigours of incubation, and to maintain temperature during the first weeks, when the long nights of early spring are still very cold. But that does not mean that the male escapes parental duties. His task is to protect the nest-site and bring in food for his patiently sitting mate, and he will also defend the nest against anything that ventures too near. In such instances, he can be entirely fearless, even when facing a much bigger animal.

The most aggressive defender on record is the **tawny owl** – I once had my scalp raked by an angry parent while checking a nest in an oak tree, and it is not an experience I wish to repeat. Both adults will drop from the sky to lash out with outstretched talons and the effects can be serious, as the invader's head is always the target. Injuries needing stitches are commonplace and people have lost eyes in extreme cases. Biologists who regularly work with owls are careful to protect themselves with hard hats and welding glasses before getting too close.

Owls usually spend the incubation period quietly. The female sits tight while the male is out looking for food. Hatching is timed to take place at the time of maximum food supply, so the male should have little problem finding prey for both himself and his mate. It is in every breeding bird's interest to produce chicks at the earliest possible part of the season. This will give the young the maximum time to prepare for winter and may even allow the adults to breed a second time, but early nesters always run a risk. Weather is not predictable and unseasonal cold or wet periods can be the death of young birds if the male cannot find enough prey to take back to the nest. Each year sees its share of dead chicks, but the built-in calendars of most adults are good enough to guarantee that there is food for most of the waiting mouths.

Tawny owl and chick

Hatching

If hatching takes place too early in the year, the food level may be too low to provide for both parents and chicks. If it is too late, there might not be enough time for the young birds to fledge and become self-sufficient before the onset of bad winter weather. This is particularly important to the owls that live in the far north, where summers are extremely short and the breeding season of their prey is correspondingly compressed.

Ideally, nesting needs to start very early in the season as raising chicks is a slow business. In the case of **barn owls** fifteen weeks can elapse from the appearance of the first egg until complete independence of the final chick. This is one of the few species that can regularly produce more than one brood in a year; barn owls in the tropics, where there is less difference between the seasons, will lay two clutches in quick succession if conditions are right, although the mortality rate is often higher in the second set of chicks.

Since the incubation time is constant, the eggs hatch in the same order as they are laid. Known as asynchronous incubation, this strongly favours the oldest chicks. In a brood of five young, there might be a difference in age of ten days between the youngest and oldest. That is a long time in the development of a bird, and the first-born can be three times heavier than the last.

Immediately after hatching, the female broods her family to keep them warm, as they cannot control their body temperature in the early days of life. Chicks in open nests have to be sheltered from wind, rain and sunshine, for without the insulating effects of thick feathers they can die of both chilling and overheating. At first the male alone has to supply food for both adults and the chicks. After a successful foray, the male simply drops the food at the nest-site and leaves to hunt again or roost in a nearby tree. His presence would be a threat to the female, particularly as food is involved.

Young owls are blind, helpless and cannot feed themselves. They must rely on their mother to tear off small strips of meat that can be swallowed whole. Like all birds, the female feeds the mouth that reaches highest and makes the most noise, and while they all stretch and call out, it is the biggest, oldest chick that always eats its fill first, followed by the second, and so on.

Unless the food supply is very good – and the male is a skilled hunter – there is rarely sufficient prey about to feed all of the chicks properly. In big broods, the youngest often become weak and stop begging for food, and so the female stops feeding them. As they become weaker and less active, the others may no longer recognise them as chicks, but see them as just another meal left by the male. And, although it might seem gruesome, they will then be eaten by the older siblings. Nothing can be wasted. This is not an accidental strategy but ensures that the strongest off-

The head is always last to get its adult feathers

spring have the best chance of survival. If the entire clutch hatched at the same time and the food was equally distributed between them, each chick might receive too little to develop properly. At least, this way, some have a good start.

Newly hatched owls have an off-white fluffy coat which later forms the underdown of their plumage. The female stays with them until the first feathers begin to form and the chicks' temperature regulation is better. She then begins hunting herself, for by now the male alone cannot meet the growing needs of the young family.

Vocally begging for food is a matter of life and death for chicks and they instinctively know that it is vitally important to be fed first, before the food runs out. Inside the deep shadows of a hollow tree they cannot see the adults return, but they can hear them. The reflex calling action is also a method of self-defence for the chicks. Owls are conditioned by instinct to eat small animals. It is in the chicks' interest to tell the adults that they are hungry offspring and not potential food. The slightest sound close to the nest entrance can trigger off the chicks' begging calls. But they are not always right. Any large bird landing on the tree can start them off, and sometimes they will call out if an animal walks underneath and brushes against the leaves. Many unsuspected owl nests inside trees are discovered through the constant, noisy calls of hungry chicks.

Youngsters in open nests do not face the same problems because they can see when their parents are coming back. The trouble is that the chicks themselves can also be seen. Baby birds offer an attractive snack to many animals and are completely defenceless if the adults are away, but owl chicks are not quite as vulnerable as they seem. Once they reach the age of about three weeks they will give warning displays to anything that comes near.

In miniature duplication of their parents, the youngsters instinctively spread their wings and beak-snap. Their small size and lack of feathers makes the sight comical to a human's eyes but a passing crow, if it is not too hungry, might well be deterred by four half-grown owls displaying aggression, and often bluff saves their lives.

Snowy owls have nests that are exposed to any passing predator, but they are powerful birds and can drive away the smaller animals. Bigger predators, however, are dealt with in a more imaginative manner. If the adults feel that danger is getting too close to the chicks they leave the nest and start a distraction display. The owl will drag one wing on the ground, feigning injury, and pretending that it can't fly. A fully grown snowy owl offers a much better meal than three tiny chicks to a hungry wolf, so it follows the adult. Slowly the 'injured' bird struggles away from the nest-site, always keeping just out of the wolf's reach but close enough to entice it steadily away from the chicks. Once the bird feels that the danger is far enough away from the nest, it drops the pretence and flies off.

Young owls begin to learn while still in the nest. As their strength and confidence grows they indulge in wing-stretching exercises to strengthen their muscles. The female gradually does less for them and eventually they have to feed themselves. After hunting, the adults bring back food and drop it, making the chicks work for their meal. At first, most try to swallow the prey whole, whatever the size, as this is the way that they have always eaten. When they find that this doesn't work, other methods have to be tried. Slowly the inexperienced birds learn to pull off small pieces, which takes some time but is a skill that must be mastered.

Feather preening takes up a big part of the day, particularly after eating. As the brood grows towards maturity, their solitary nature shows itself. Squabbles and disputes break out over nothing, which result in talon-tangling fights and much beak snapping. The nest soon becomes too small for the young birds.

Leaving the nest

Chicks reared inside holes first leave the security of their nest long before they can fly. They sit on nearby branches, stretching their wings and dozing, only to dart back inside if danger threatens. All owls seem to enjoy sunbathing, particularly after a cold night, and when a shaft of sunlight hits the nest they face into it, close their eyes and spread their wings to take in the maximum amount of heat. Their behaviour is not all that different from holidaymakers on the beach. A well-fed owl will frequently bask in the sun throughout its life, although it can overheat on very hot days.

From their nest the young owls learn to watch and listen, sharpening their senses ready for self-sufficiency. Most young birds leave the nest for good before they can fly properly, but, as they go through early test flights and crash landings, honing their aerial skills, their parents still bring in prey and take it to the scattered family. Gradually the parents withdraw the food and, for the first time, the young owls must fend for themselves.

There is a myth that all predators can instinctively hunt and kill. They cannot. Just like a baby learning to walk, hunting is a technique that is not instantly attained, it must be practised and perfected. The only difference is that, if a baby cannot walk immediately it simply falls over, whereas if the young owl fails to master hunting, it dies.

All chicks are endowed with the instinct to watch and kill, but they do not know precisely how to do it. Hunting is a learning process, a matter of trial and error to discover where the prey can be found, what to eat and how exactly to catch it. Young owls supplement their diet with invertebrates, such as worms and beetles, while they explore and discover the subtleties of hunting. Many fail every year. Inexperienced birds that do not learn quickly, die of starvation. This is a good example of natural selection and ensures that only the most able, efficient hunters pass on their genes to the next generation.

Life is harsh for newly fledged owls. While mastering flight they can fall prey to foxes, cats and a host of other ground-based predators. The mortality rate can be as high as 70 per cent in the first six months. As if this wasn't enough to contend with, the young owls have to compete directly with their parents for food and space. Once the adults stop feeding their family, the young become rivals in the heart of their territory and must be driven away. A suitable, unoccupied area has to be found before winter.

Young males feel an instinct to find and protect a nest-site, ready for the breeding season of the following spring. The vast majority of owls breed in their first spring, barely a year after leaving the protection of their parents.

6 The Solitary Life

By midsummer the most recent batch of young owls has left the nest-site, the pair-bonds have broken and the birds involved have gone their own way. The weather and food supply are both still good, so life settles down. With the number of prey animals at its seasonal highest, hunting poses no difficulties. After eating their fill, owls will often bathe in shallow pools on warm nights. They don't go beneath the surface but lie on their fronts, splashing with spread wings and dipping their heads into the water. Wet owls, however, are vulnerable creatures; soaked in water their weight increases and their feathers do not work properly, so they must find a place of safety where they can sleep and dry off.

Roosting

Above all else, roosting owls want peace. They choose well-hidden corners where they can spend the daylight hours dozing. **Barn owls** have favourite spots that are used every day, **tawnies** just pick a suitable tree.

Tawny owl roosting

The colour of most owls tells us that they are woodland birds. The endless permutations of brown, grey and black combine to form perfect camouflage against the subdued, dappled light in a forest. Roosting owls, therefore, are terribly difficult to find. With feathers fluffed out, sitting motionless close to the trunk, they look like part of the tree. Owls do not sleep with their heads tucked under a wing, they just pull one leg up into the thick layer of feathers and their head sinks down a little. Occasionally the owl will wake, change legs and have a look around. They will wake immediately at the sound of any approaching animal, but, with their eyes open to a slit, they still seem to sleep. Owls have complete confidence in the quality of their camouflage and although an unwary owl might be taken by an agile pine marten or goshawk, the generally watchful birds hold their ground, even when humans come close.

When real danger looms, roosting owls opt for discretion rather than flight. Many small owls emphasise their camouflage by pulling in their feathers and stretching upwards. This is called **stiffening** and makes the owl seem much thinner and even more like an old branch. Their faces 'close down', making them look less like owls, and they assume an expression that has been described as looking as if they have been sucking lemons. The change happens instantly and is a remarkable transformation.

Barn owl with closed facial discs

Mobbing

Predators, however, are not the only hazards to a sleeping owl. Strangely, they may be severely pestered by much smaller antagonists. The most important element of a predator's attack is surprise. The sudden appearance confuses a prey animal and consequently its reaction is slower. It logically follows, therefore, that a predator which is seen in advance loses its advantage. Should a foraging **blackbird** accidentally spot a tawny owl sleeping in a tree, it pours out a strident danger call that can be translated by all other local birds. Soon several species join together to shout shrill warning calls, while rapidly opening and closing their wings and flicking their tails in an agitated show of defiance. Hopping from branch to branch they quickly attract passing birds and all join in the general harassment of the roosting tawny.

In most cases the owl seems completely oblivious to the chaos it is causing – its eyes stay tightly closed and there is no movement – but the dozing predator is perfectly aware of what is happening. The owl simply wants to be left in peace and, at first, refuses to leave. The screaming birds gradually become more daring and will dart to within talon-striking distance but, even then, the owl remains unmoved. If the owl were hunting, the birds would be taking a very grave risk; but they seem to realise that, when roosting, it poses no real threat. The reaction to the owl is very different from that created by a hunter that specialises in catching small birds. Sparrowhawks, for example, have the speed and agility to take predatorial advantage of a mobbing and are simply too dangerous to treat this way.

The object of the performance is to make life so uncomfortable for the owl that it will move on. All owls have to become accustomed to this treatment and they will tolerate it for a considerable time. They will occasionally leave if the irritating commotion becomes persistent but, as they would have to fly in daylight, they are just as likely to be seen by other birds and receive a similar reception at their next roost-site.

After a while, the mobbing birds slowly lose enthusiasm and return to feeding. The exercise, however, is of real survival value to the smaller birds, and for days afterwards all the birds that took part in the mobbing will studiously avoid the roost-site, even if the owl has long gone.

Interestingly, the vociferousness and determination of the mobbing birds is inversely proportional to their size. Every spring, swallows breed in my studio. When they arrive we leave a small window open for them and they build their mud nest high on an old oak beam. One day, shortly after their chicks had hatched, I was due to give a talk to a bird club and Rocky, my tame eagle owl, was coming along with me. She was sitting quietly on her log, close to the studio door, when the swallows returned to feed their young. Without hesitation they started to dive-bomb the owl. Each of the birds flew directly at her head, actually hitting her about 50 per cent of the time. Rocky just crouched lower and lower as the birds swooped relentlessly. She made no attempt to retaliate, she simply tried to duck, and in the end she lay flat on her thick branch with eyes closed and an air of resigned suffering. Even when I picked her up, the angry swallows wouldn't stop. They flew within inches of my head as I carried the eagle owl to the car. When she was safely inside, with the doors closed, the swallows obviously felt that they had conscientiously

Barn owl

The scientific name for this Tengmalm's owl is Aegolius funereus – the unlucky owl

completed their job. They sat on the overhead telegraph wire and twittered, while Rocky sat inside the car and preened, something that most owls do when they have been disturbed or frightened.

The instinct to mob is very strong amongst small birds. Experiments have shown that it does not even take a live owl to stimulate the response. A badly stuffed specimen left in a tree will bring forth an angry mobbing flock. It used to be thought that an owl's eyes were the most provocative part of its anatomy until people realised that roosting owls have their eyes closed. Now we know that it is the characteristic round head and upright posture that first alerts the birds. Should an unwise owl open its eyes, however, the degree of mobbing dramatically increases. For tawnies, with their deep brown eyes, the increase is relatively small, but long-eared owls, with their distinctive orange irises, have a truly miserable time. Tightly closed eyes are as much a safety mechanism as a show of indifference.

Mobbing has been known and understood by man for many centuries and used to his advantage. A captive owl, such as the **eagle owl** in Europe and the **great horned** in North America, would be tethered to the ground in an open space but close to trees or shrubs. The mobbing instinct is at its strongest when the owl is first seen, and within minutes small birds arrived to scold and shout. What happened then depended upon the intentions of the waiting men. Some hunters used the technique to bring birds within the range of their guns, but shooting was considered to be a counter-productive method as the loud noise of the gunshot would deter others from joining in. Bird lime was a popular alternative. This highly sticky substance was painted on to branches and twigs around the decoy owl, and once the birds landed on them, they were held fast. In many countries, birds were a vital – and free – source of meat; a large owl was a valuable asset that could provide food for several days.

On busy days the lime would have to be replaced hourly. The best time for this activity was during the migration periods of spring and autumn, when countless birds were passing through. Then the daily catches could be measured in hundreds, just with one owl. Falconers used the same ploy to trap birds of prey because hawks and falcons will also mob large owls. Instead of using lime, however, the falconers used fine nets to capture their prey live and relatively unharmed.

Migration

Migration probably evolved as a way of avoiding food shortages in the winter months. If the food supply is plentiful and constant, then there is no need to move away. Long-distance flights require an enormous amount of energy and the potential hazards are considerable. Migrants face strange weather conditions, new predators and the difficulties of finding food in a completely unknown environment. Small birds are not the only ones to migrate, although owls certainly cannot be regarded as great travellers. Most are stay-at-home types that rarely travel more than 30 kilometres from where they were born. There are, though, seasonal movements inside a territory – for instance, many owls move down to a lower altitude during the winter – and some species do undertake ambitious flights.

Insect-eating species are the hardest hit in the winter, for then their prey all but disappears and they must move on to more profitable hunting grounds. The insectivorous **scops owls** breed in southern Europe, where they stay until late summer. But in autumn they move down to Africa where insects can still be found. The **saw-whet owl** of North America has an annual migration journey of around 2400 kilometres, an amazing achievement for a bird that is not designed for long-distance travel. Although it does not cover as much distance, the migration of the tiny **elf owl** is an equally remarkable feat. It makes the yearly return flight from the scrublands of the USA to an unknown destination in Central America.

Some owls do not migrate in the conventional sense, their movements are more random and erratic. **Dispersals**, as they are known, are not fully understood but they do provide impressive statistics. I was recently talking to an ornithologist who, on a windy November afternoon, found a long-eared owl sitting on a beach in Lincolnshire. The bird was wearing a German ring and must have flown across the North Sea. It was discovered huddled just above the tide-line on the first solid landing site it had seen and was so exhausted that it could be picked up and examined without the slightest struggle. It was kept in a recovery pen for forty-eight hours, fed well and then released.

During the winter of 1945-6 no fewer than 13,502 **snowy owls** from the Canadian Arctic appeared on the eastern coast of America. They all seemed to be very hungry – one attacked and carried off a squirrel's tail tied to a car's radio aerial, another made repeated swoops on to the furry hat of a game warden.

These mass movements of snowy owls are called **invasions** or **irruptions** and take place about once every four years. They coincide with poor breeding seasons for their main prey of lemmings, then the owls are forced south to find alternative food. Young snowy owls will travel vast distances while searching for a suitable territory. They may be arctic specialists but odd birds have turned up as far south as the Azores, Bermuda and even Pakistan.

I once witnessed a mass winter gathering of snowy owls in Canada. I heard via the unofficial owl-grapevine that they were flocking in to take advantage of a vole plague on the tiny inland island of Amhurst in Lake Ontario; so, with Keith Offord, a fellow

Previous page *Great grey owl*

Above *Boobook owl in flight*

Left *Grass owls have unusually long legs for snatching food out of deep undergrowth*

Above left *The burrowing owl spends much of its life at ground level*

Above right *The ferruginous pygmy, from central and south America, is one of the world's smallest owls*

Left *Snowy owls are perfectly camouflaged for life in cold climates*

Above left *The great horned owl is the largest owl on the American continent*

Above right *Ural owls live in the woodlands of northern Europe and Asia*

Left *The collared scops owl lives in Asia, where they feed on insects and have even been seen to catch bats in flight*

strigiphile (owl lover), I quickly booked a flight to go and see for myself.

The flat, sparsely populated island is a quiet place and the landscape is dominated by large ungrazed fields. Even the expression 'plague' could not begin to describe the hordes of voles that over-ran the island, for each footstep would disturb three or four of the small animals and send them scurrying to shelter. Much of Amhurst was blanketed in deep snow and the voles tended to stay in the few open, ice-free areas. The temperature was appallingly low, at midday the air measured -20°C.

But the attraction of the voles overcame any dislike of the cold that might be felt by hungry predators. Amhurst had long been free of large earth-bound animals, and birds were the only carnivores that were sufficiently mobile to move in and plunder the small mammals. Red-tailed hawks, northern harriers and rough-legged buzzards floated lazily over the grass. Over one vole-rich pasture there were eight short-eared owls carefully searching for food. These airborne hunters were clearly visible against the dull winter skies. But the immaculately camouflaged snowy owls were far more elusive. Try as we might we could not see a single owl, despite reports that they were 'everywhere'. An hour after landing on the island I wandered on to the stony beach with a pair of binoculars to scan the ice floes, when behind came Keith's quiet, insistent voice: 'Mike, there's a snowy

During the vole plague on Amhurst Island, snowy owls perched, well fed, on telegraph poles

behind you.'

It sat on a low fence post just twenty metres away, blending perfectly with the icy background. There is a definite knack needed to detect a snowy owl on home ground, the colour-match is immaculate and they sit absolutely motionless with their eyes closed to mere slits to keep out the glare reflected by the bright snow. It is the shape that gives the bird away.

Once we had seen three or four, the task became simple. Suddenly there were snowy owls everywhere, as there had been since we arrived – only now we could see them. The great white owls perched on telegraph poles, bird boxes and even roofs. Each would sit for up to half an hour, then pounce on to the frozen earth to catch a vole. With so much prey about, the owls were not having to work hard. I was very keen to photograph a snowy in its most suitable habitat, so I set off quietly across the ice to stalk a sleeping one. I tried at least ten times, the owl watching me through hooded eyes, waiting until I got within 30 metres, then flying further out on to the frozen lake. Like all owls, it felt more vulnerable on the ground. Sitting on a high telegraph pole, it was safe from wildlife photographers below; it was not so confident on the open ice when we were at the same level.

Most of the hunting owls were relatively unconcerned by the presence of humans. As I stalked towards them with a camera, they would stare with beautiful gold-and-black eyes that grew wider as I approached. They would then rise and wheel off to sit on another post to resume their search. I did find one male that was not the least bit worried. I stood at the bottom of a telegraph pole while he sat at the top, peering down. Unfortunately, this viewpoint was not ideal for photogra-phy, as I could only see the underside of the owl, which is not the most flattering view of any animal. We found one male sitting on a wooden post that was holding up a clothes line in the back garden of a house close to the shore. Just a few metres away was a huge labrador, chained to a heavy kennel. The dog was distinctly unhappy about the owl's pres-ence, but although the frantic barking would have driven away the most determined of human intruders, the snowy owl held its ground and studied the long grass for move-ment. It sat for more than fifteen minutes as the dog barked and pulled on its chain; with-out warning the owl then dropped into the long grass, emerged with a vole and returned to the safety of the ice. After three days of watching on Amhurst Island, I became blasé but, looking back, the first sight of a wild snowy is one of the most memorable events of my owl career.

In any group of animals there are always individual species that break the usual rules, and owls are no exception. While most owls rarely migrate, the **great grey** is a natural nomad. Its nesting behaviour is closely relat-ed to the presence of voles and they rear their young in areas with the best supply of these rodents. Outside the breeding season they scatter in all directions and there are mass movements in autumn and winter. Should the owls find a suitable territory during their travels, they are quite likely to stay and breed in the spring.

Tengmalm's owls even have different behaviour patterns according to their sex. Males may remain on territory all year round, while the females and young birds disperse. These birds lay their eggs in abandoned woodpecker holes, which are highly valued commodities in coniferous forests. Whenever migratory birds return to their breeding grounds they have to battle for temporary ownership of good territories; but the male Tengmalm's owl, who protects his home ground all year round, does not have to endure this and is ready and waiting, with an established nest-site, for the return of the female in spring. This is convenient for the male birds and valuable for the welfare of the species as a whole, since the nest-hole is safeguarded not only against other types of owl but also from small birds and squirrels. The breeding den might be secured but individual males do suffer when it comes to hunting. The females leave because food becomes scarce; however, with half of the species departing, there is less competition for the remaining prey.

7 British Owls

Britain has six residential species of owl although one, the **snowy**, is only just about hanging on here and could soon be joining the list of occasional visitors. Species from mainland Europe pop up at irregular intervals, **Tengmalm's**, **common scops** and **hawk owls** have all been seen in recent years.

It's been said many times before, but it is worth repeating that, for a small island, Britain has a remarkable diversity in its physical landscape. The mixture of ancient woodlands, conifer forests, moor and marshes, traditional agricultural land, beaches and even town suburbs, provides a rich and attractive cross-section of habitats for wildlife. Environments in the temperate zone can never compete with the tropics for the range of species and sheer number of animals but, as a small northerly group of islands, Britain does quite well.

In owl history, however, Britain was once even better off. The remains of both **Tengmalm's** and **hawk owl**, dating back to the last Ice Age, have been found in the Midlands.

Bones of European **eagle owls** have also been discovered but, as they would have been a predator of domestic livestock, they became extinct long before the Middle Ages as the result of over-hunting. There is a movement to reintroduce these giants into the more remote parts of the British countryside and, in theory at least, this could be easily done. Eagle owls reproduce well in captivity and breed-and-release schemes have been successfully carried out in Germany, Norway and other parts of Europe. But reintroduction is not simply a matter of opening a cage and letting the birds fly. They must have a reasonable chance of survival. In his book *Owls of the Northern Hemisphere*, Professor Karel Voous says that 'in some senses the Eurasian Eagle Owl is now a bird of the past'.

These birds evolved for life in uncluttered habitats; man, with his complex road systems, cultivated land and endless buildings, has made eagle owls rare throughout most of Europe. Invariably, whenever man begins to control the landscape, it is always the bigger animals that suffer first for they need the most space and food. They are also the most obvious targets for hunters. In addition, the population of the large mammals which form part of the eagle owl's diet has been vanishing over the past 500 years and the owls are now taking smaller animals than their ancestors. They will hunt for any prey animal that offers a convenient meal, but there are precious few places in the wilder parts of Britain that are far from a sheep farm, and the temptation for introduced owls to hunt lambs would be impossible to control. To quote Voous again: 'Such a large and powerful predator as the Eurasian eagle owl can hardly be expected to succeed in adapting itself to a life permanently close to human civilisation, let alone find its required variety of prey there.'

All attempts to release eagle owls have so far been blocked by the Government, and most biologists hope that this policy remains unchanged. The introduction of a massive predator into an established environment could be disastrous for the existing animals – as well as for the owls themselves.

Exact information on owl numbers in the past is impossible to find, as biological recorders were haphazard and unreliable, but it's probably fair to say that, with the exception of the little owl, which didn't appear until recently, all the species that now inhabit Britain were once a lot more common. It does not take an expert to realise that human activities have been the cause of this

Barn owl with its characteristic, heart-shaped face

drop in numbers. During the years between 1900 and 1950 more land was built upon than had been in the whole of British history until then. Not only did this building marathon gobble up a vast area of land, it also needed a huge quantity of wood, sand, gravel and other natural resources and the resulting loss of habitat was on a scale that had never before been experienced.

Some animals are highly adaptable and can settle down to life with man. Mammals, reptiles, butterflies and a growing list of small birds now make their permanent home in urban and suburban areas. The creation of parks, gardens, roadside verges and the other by-products of development has suited them. In dozens of town centres, generations of foxes have made a fine living, hunting mice and scavenging off waste food. Not all species, though, can readjust their life styles

Fledgling tawny owl learning to fend for itself

so comprehensively. **Tawny owls** have made the move successfully, but the more wary **long-eareds** probably never will.

The biggest danger facing Britain's wildlife is no longer direct persecution, it is the destruction of its habitat. Owls are legally protected against hunting and egg-collecting, with penalties for offenders who are caught. But these laws are virtually meaningless if developers are free to fell the nesting trees and pave over grassland where owls have hunted for hundreds of years. To be really effective, the law should safeguard all aspects of the owl's life; a hunting ban is important but of limited use if the forests and meadows that supply food are not given equal protection.

Yet it is not all doom and gloom for owls in Britain. The six British owls – tawny, long-eared, short-eared, little, snowy and barn owl – continue to thrive in certain places and some are even extending their range.

Tawny owl (*Strix aluco*)

	Female	Male
Average weight	600g	450g
Average wingspan	100cm	94cm
Average length	45cm	42cm

Food: Mainly wood mouse, shrew and field vole. Also brown rat, bank vole, young rabbit, mole, weasel. Occasionally robin, greenfinch, newt, frog and fish.

UK range: Throughout mainland Britain, absent from northern Scotland and all of Ireland.

World distribution: Central and southern Europe, parts of Asia.

Breeding: Nests in hollow trees, nest boxes, abandoned nests of other species; does not line the nest. Breeding activity begins in late March in the south but slightly later in northern areas. 2-4 eggs, maximum 8. Incubation 28-30 days. Young leave nest at 5 weeks old.

The tawny, also called the **brown owl** or **wood owl**, is the archetypal owl of European culture. Whenever stylised owls are portrayed in books, adverts or anywhere else that does not require biological accuracy, the tawny owl is inevitably shown. They are the most widespread and numerous of all British owls and their population has been steadily increasing over the past fifty years. Despite a few attempts to introduce tawny owls into Ireland, they have never become established there. Tawnies are not natural travellers and would never normally attempt to cross an expanse of water the size of the Irish Sea. Their traditional habitat is **mature deciduous woodland** but they are known to be highly flexible and can now be found living in town parks, suburbia and even coniferous forests. One pair of Scottish owls raised their family inside an abandoned car.

One reason for the recent success of tawny

owls is probably their relationship with man. To put it simply, they seem to ignore us unless we pose a direct threat. Many species will keep away from built-up areas instinctively, in favour of a human-free environment, but tawnies will happily move in anywhere providing there are suitable breeding and hunting sites. This means that they are free to exploit new, unoccupied territories without facing competition. It is now possible to stand in the centre of London at night and listen to the calls of resident tawny owls coming from several directions.

The name 'tawny' refers to their brown plumage, which has evolved as cryptic camouflage for woodlands, but some individual birds look much more grey. The colour difference in this species is mainly governed by geography – tawnies from eastern Europe and Asia tend to be grey while their British counterparts are usually brown. Grey tawny owls do regularly crop up in Britain – they might look like a completely different species, but they are simply displaying a variation in colour and can breed with the more conventionally coloured owls. Such variation in colour is known as **dimorphism** and is controlled by genes; the ability to produce individuals with different shades of plumage increases the possibility of the species adapting its camouflage to a wider range of habitats.

Tawnies are mainly **nocturnal**, which explains why they are so rarely seen, but they will hunt during the day when extra food has to be found for chicks. They may emerge in the daytime but even then these owls hunt inside the dark shadows of a woodland canopy. This behaviour helps to explain why tawnies are so rarely seen even though they are the most numerous of British owls. Sightings are usually confined to quick glimpses showing the silhouette of a sitting bird on a branch or telegraph pole in the dull afterglow of dusk. Some people only see tawnies caught for a second in car headlights as they swoop low over a country road at night.

Unlike some species tawnies do not always return to a single favourite day-roost, but will sleep anywhere that is safe and warm inside the boundaries of their territory. Hollow trees, empty buildings and deep within the cover of dense leaves are the best places to look for sleeping tawnies. One has even been recorded roosting in a remote telephone box, having entered the kiosk through a broken pane of glass. The unpredictable habits of tawny owls make them more difficult to find; as even their pellets are usually dropped in flight and are therefore well scattered.

Most ornithologists accept that the efficiency of a tawny owl's eyesight is as good as theoretically possible for their particular design of eye. This, coupled with very acute hearing, makes them awesomely skilled nocturnal hunters. They also keep inside their heads an up-to-date, highly detailed map of their surroundings; they appear to remember the

Tawny owl with dead rabbit

the best memories of any living animal, possibly even better than a dog's. Knowing their territory is so important to the hunting success of tawny owls that they rarely, if ever, leave the area.

After the eagle owl, tawnies are the most prolific owl-killing owl in Europe, and are known to hunt at least six different species. But they have also been recorded taking kestrels, sparrowhawks and even the swift and powerful goshawk. Their staple diet, however, is not usually so dramatic or challenging to catch, and one of their favourite foods seems to be moles. In the summer, young moles are forced to travel above ground to escape from their aggressive parents and find a suitable empty territory of their own. They move at night and tawny owls quickly pick off the slow-moving animals as they crawl noisily over the grass or leaves. Moles are heavy, chunky animals and just one is worth four or five mice to an owl.

Tawnies are, without doubt, the **noisiest of British owls** – they will hoot, shriek and call all through the year, usually from a high perch. Outside my studio there is a telegraph pole and almost every night, an hour or so after sunset, the vague shape of a tawny owl can be seen as it sits and warns off rivals for ten minutes. This prompts nearby owls into song and they enthusiastically respond, with the calls echoing backwards and forwards until there is no mistake over which territories are occupied.

exact whereabouts of each tree and shrub. This intimate knowledge is extremely useful when flying beneath the dark, leafy canopy of a woodland in summer. Negotiating unfamiliar obstacles under such conditions would test the skills and sight of even a tawny owl and hunting would suffer. One researcher, with detailed information to back up his claim, has categorically said that tawny owls have one of

Tales of the ferocious attacks made by tawny owls defending nests are common and do not need to be exaggerated for effect. They will dive-bomb cats, dogs and even horses that get too close. Many public parks have had to be closed in spring when nesting tawny owls make them too dangerous to enter.

Long-eared owl (*Asio otus*)

	Female	Male
Average weight	340g	280g
Average wingspan	92.5cm	89.5cm
Average length	38.5cm	36cm

Food Field vole and young rat, also bat, lizard, frog, insects and small birds.

UK range: Throughout the country, apart from built-up areas.

World distribution: North America, Europe, northern Asia and parts of North Africa.

Breeding: In abandoned nests of other birds, such as crows, jays and other members of that family, in woodland or small copses. Occasionally on the ground or in low vegetation. Starts early March. Clutches consist of 3 or 4 eggs, maximum 8, laid on alternate days. Incubation period lasts around 28 days and young leave the nest at 24 days old.

Until the eighteenth century this species bore the name 'horn-owl', but then so did the short-eared. To prevent confusion the birds were given new but inaccurate names. I have often had minor disagreements with 'non-owlers' over the size of long-eared owls. These birds have the unique ability to look much bigger in photographs and drawings than they do in real life. I've lost count of the number of times that Rocky, my eagle owl, has been accused of being a long-eared owl by new acquaintances. 'It *is*,' they cry, 'I've seen a picture of one.' Disregarding size, long-eareds do bear more than a passing resemblance to eagle owls, since their shape, eye colour and ear tufts are very similar; but there the likeness ends. The two groups are not even closely related. To give an idea of relative size, the body weight of a long-eared owl is about an eighth of the weight of an eagle owl. Long-eareds are far smaller than most people believe, being only slightly over half the weight of a tawny owl.

There is a very good reason for this confusion. Since they are **completely nocturnal** and lack the tawny owl's blasé attitude to humans, long-eared owls are rarely seen. Their habitat is undisturbed woodland; in Britain they usually prefer conifer forests but elsewhere they will live in deciduous woods. Parks and gardens are avoided, as is suburbia. Houses are not generally built in fir-tree plantations, so long-eared owls rarely come into direct contact with man, in fact they take pains to avoid us and in many ways are the most elusive of the British owls.

Long-eared owls prefer the edges of

The large wings of a long-eared owl give it an effortless, moth-like flight

conifer woods rather than the centre where there is little ground vegetation and hardly any small mammals. During the day they sleep among the thickest parts of a tree's canopy – they are one of the few species that will **roost communally**, with groups of twenty or thirty having been seen dozing close together on summer days. Each bird has its own particular perch and likes to return to it every morning. They do not venture out until after dusk and are well equipped for a nocturnal life. Long-eareds can hunt in absolute darkness as they have one of the keenest hearing senses of any owl. With long wings and a lightweight body the wing-loading is extremely low and their flight is so buoyant that they look like giant moths as they glide between the moonlit trees.

On silent wings they search the area around the woodland edge for small animals, rarely going far into the forest or out into open ground. In winter they will sometimes prey on sleeping birds by flying close to the roost and hovering there for a short time to frighten the birds into movement and into their waiting talons. Although the catch-rate is not high, small species such as sparrows, greenfinches and thrushes are frequently killed and eaten. During bad weather starlings roost in huge numbers in reed beds or conifers, huddling together to keep warm. These sites, if found, are irresistible to hungry long-eared owls. When it comes to hunting rights, these owls are not at all territorial;

Long-eared owls hunt around the woodland edge, rarely going far into the forest to look for food

if the food supply dries up they simply move on to a new area. For owls, they are great **travellers** and often fly considerable distances in winter. They move south during very cold weather, flying independently or in small flocks. Many long-eared owls migrate to Britain when the weather in mainland Europe becomes too severe; they have been seen perching on boats in the middle of the

North Sea, taking a short, well-earned rest while negotiating the wide expanse of water. Every year, while crossing the sea, an unknown number must die in winter storms as they are blown off course and far from the safety of land. Owls are not powerful fliers and are at the mercy of strong winds. On land this is just an inconvenience, over the sea it can be fatal.

Migrant long-eared owls are often found coated in a foul-smelling oil which is squirted at them, in self-defence, by fulmars. These seabirds roost in huge numbers on cliff-faces which, as they are usually the first dry land to be seen, are frequently the landing point of the tired owls. The fulmars, alarmed at the sudden appearance of a predator, react by violently expelling a jet of oil from their mouths directly at the owl. This is done with some force as the oil can hit a target up to a metre away. If the owl is lucky it escapes before the whole colony joins in. If it is too slow the feathers become soaked and heavy so the bird cannot fly. In early winter countless long-eared owls die as a result of fulmar attacks.

In Britain, long-eareds are still sometimes called **horned** or **tufted owls**; in America they are known as **cat owls** because of their pointed ears and silent habits. They may be quiet in flight but long-eared owls are quite capable of making noises. Their seldom-used call has been described as sounding like a 'depressed moaning'. The steady 'poop – poop – poop' is used mostly during the breeding season, but researchers have made a list of twenty-three other distinct sounds made by these owls.

Of Britain's fifty-six million acres, only four million are forested; and just a quarter of this is made up of coniferous woodland. Since the beginning of the twentieth century the number of long-eared owls has slowly dropped, not dramatically, but in a steady, determined way. One theory is that they are being ousted by the larger and more aggressive tawny owls; long-eareds do well in Ireland, where there are no tawnies. But there are big loopholes in this argument. Tawnies and long-eareds have always lived alongside each other and, although they compete for similar food, they have different nesting needs and tawnies have a strong preference for deciduous woods.

The real truth is that we don't exactly know why the population of long-eared owls is dropping. Man's activities in the countryside, and subsequent disturbances to the resident wildlife, must play a part; but most conifer forests are dull in our eyes and are mainly overlooked, apart from logging operations. Even then, until the trees are commercially mature, they are left more or less alone.

There is a small-scale project currently under way to help these owls by supplying extra nest-sites. In a few, well-guarded locations, wicker baskets have been attached to trees at 'long-eared' level, to give the owls a sturdy platform that will hold their eggs.

Some have been used but it is still too early to say if this idea will help the species in the long term. The mystery of the long-eareds' dilemma is just another field of owl ecology that we still do not understand.

Little owl (*Athene noctua*)

	Female	Male
Average weight	180g	160g
Average wingspan	50cm	47.5cm
Average length	21.5cm	19cm

Food: Earthworm, beetle, moth, grasshopper, also small mammals such as voles, etc.

UK range: Throughout England and Wales. Absent from northern Scotland and all of Ireland.

World distribution: Central and southern Europe, Middle East, Central Asia and North Africa.

Breeding: Nests in hollow trees, dry-stone walls, nest boxes and even holes in the ground; does not line the nest. Starts in mid-April. 3-5 eggs, maximum 8. Incubation 28 days. Young leave the nest at 28 days and can fly well at 35 days old.

A hundred and fifty years ago this section would have been impossible to include, for then the little owl was a rare novelty that few people had seen in Britain. In fact these birds are not native to British shores, for their true and original home is mainland Europe.

Although the species may have been present in prehistoric times, its first recent appearance took place on 10 May 1842. Charles Waterton, squire of Walton Hall in Yorkshire, bought twelve *civettas* (little owls) from a market trader in Rome; he thought that they would make a fine addition to the birdlife around his house. Seven died on the journey to England and the remaining five were released to fend for themselves on the large estate. They were never seen again.

Several other half-hearted attempts were made to introduce little owls, but the responsibility for the final success can be laid at the feet of Thomas Powys, Fourth Baron Lilford. In 1888 he released forty imported birds on his estate near Oundle in Northamptonshire. Here they found a near-perfect habitat and were carefully nurtured by staff, who were under strict instructions to encourage the small visitors. From Lilford Park they quickly spread into the surrounding countryside until they occupied most of the southeast of England. Their numbers were constantly reinforced by fresh owls that were imported and released by other interested landowners. The speed of their colonisation was incredible by any conventional standard. Because there was no resident owl of that size, little owls had no direct competition for food or nesting-sites. They were filling an ecological niche that was previously empty, a rare situation in any established habitat. With few controlling influences, they were free to breed at maximum speed.

By the 1930s little owls had become an almost common inhabitant, but there was plenty of controversy over their presence. Many people welcomed the birds as a harmless, attractive and unique addition to the countryside, while others condemned them as vicious killers of young pheasants and partridges. Gamekeepers wanted the little owl to be legally classified as vermin, so that they could be hunted and finally eliminated from Britain. The debate became fierce and raged for several years until the BTO (British Trust for Ornithology) stepped in to end the argument once and for all, scientifically. In 1935 they commissioned a Miss Alison Hibbert-Ware to investigate the diet of little owls to establish exactly what they were eating. Over the next eighteen months, she carried out a thorough analysis of their feeding habits. She examined the contents of 76 nests, did autopsies on 28 dead owls to look at their stomach contents and carefully scrutinised 2460 pellets. These were collected from various parts of the country, including places where game birds were intensively reared. After this painstaking task, she uncovered evidence of only two game birds that had been eaten, which represented a tiny percentage of the little owls' diet, considering the huge amount of material that had been studied.

The survey showed that, far from being merciless killers of pheasants and partridges, little owls were mainly insect-eaters. The remains of 10,217 earwigs were found, 343 in one pellet alone, and they also contained bits of beetles, moths and earthworms. The most favourable piece of evidence was the fact that the owls were shown to eat a huge number of crane-fly larvae, the 'leatherjackets' that cause so much damage to farm crops. Eventually even the most ardent critics had to admit that the introduction of the little owl probably did more good than harm, at least from the landowners' point of view.

Yet the results of the Hibbert-Ware survey were slightly misleading, as only about half of the little owl's diet consists of insects. For their size, they are **aggressive and powerful hunters**, capable of killing something as large as a young rat. One census showed that the average weight of a **barn owl's** kill (measuring small mammals only) was 23.6g, while the average for the much smaller **little owl** was 32.1g, which represented one-fifth of its own body weight. These birds are true opportunists and one of the least specialised of owls; their eyesight and hearing are not particularly sharp when compared with nocturnal masters such as the tawny owl and are only fractionally better than the similar-sized blackbird, a species that hunts in daylight.

Little owls are not nocturnal but **crepuscular**, which means that they prefer to be active around dusk and dawn. Today they can be found on farmland, in orchards and even cemeteries; they are sedentary birds and tend to stay in one area throughout their life. Little

Little owls can often be seen during the day, sitting on fence posts

owl territories are very small and youngsters often take up residence just a few hundred metres from where they hatched. During bad weather conditions they are likely to die of starvation rather than move on. Lack of specialisation means that little owls can exploit a wide range of foods, while more fastidious species suffer badly when their particular prey is hard to find.

Unlike most other species, little owl chicks hatch at more or less the same time, for with such a wide-ranging diet there is usually enough food to share amongst a big family. A heavy reliance on insects, however, does cause problems when snow lies deep on the ground because little owls are not strong or heavy enough to break through a thick layer, and they suffer terribly in long, cold winters. They are birds that thrive in warmer, southern climates and they will never do well in the harsh, northern temperatures. In cold conditions, little owls fluff out their feathers and become so round that they look like an entirely different species, the thickened plumage acting like a duvet and helping to keep them warm. At the slightest sound of danger, however, they rapidly resume their normal streamline shape, ready for action.

With just a little patience, little owls are the most visible and approachable of all the native species. The effort is worthwhile, for these are entertaining birds. They can often be seen in daylight perching on high lookout points, such as fence posts and telegraph poles, watching for prey on the ground below. Moving slowly and carefully, it is possible to get quite near but, with each step, the owl gets increasingly agitated and frantically bobs its head up and down before it panics and flies off.

Little owls have a distinctive undulating flight that takes a lot of effort and they often close their wings for an instant and glide to save energy. Close up, these owls have a different appearance from other British species. They are the **smallest owls in the country** and have a squat, stumpy shape with a strange, flat-topped head. The bright yellow iris gives the bird a fierce expression which, in my experience, is an accurate reflection of its temperament. Little owls have a low, explosive call that is far from musical; in fact, in Europe this eerie sound has earned them the title 'bird of death'.

My own first contact with a little owl took place while sitting in a hide trying to photograph kingfishers. The canvas tent was built on a rocky riverbed carved deep into a Shropshire field. As I sat waiting for the kingfishers to return to their nest, I could see the top of the grassy bank at eye level just two metres from me. It was only an hour after dawn which is the best time to photograph nesting birds as the chicks are hungry following the long cold night and the adults feed them more often. Between kingfisher visits I sat looking out of the tiny peephole in the canvas.

Suddenly I saw a small, round face peering over the long grass near the top of the bank. It was there for just a second and soon disappeared. Up it popped again, this time in a different place, quickly looked around and then ducked down. Little owls often hunt for insects on foot, but in long grass they have to be wary for they are small and can fall prey to a wide range of bigger predators. When the vegetation is tall they frequently stop to look for potential danger. Two or three times a minute the small head would briefly appear, glance around and vanish. I was intrigued and wanted to see more; so I picked up two small stones and tapped them together. The effect was just as I had hoped. Not only did the head spring up but the entire top half of the owl's body came into view as it stretched as high as possible to search for the source of the sound. As I tapped, the owl bobbed and weaved, staring directly at the hide but unable to see any movement. Finally it could stand no more and flew away.

After a very uncertain start, little owls are now part of Britain's birdlife. Most landowners welcome them, throughout Europe, for their part in controlling insect pests. The population seems to be slowly dropping, but this might be a natural fluctuation that occurs occasionally in all species. Most introduced animals have had a disastrous effect on the countryside, but little owls are an exception. They have fitted into their new homeland with barely a ripple; long may they remain.

Short-eared owl (*Asio flammeus*)

	Female	Male
Average weight	410g	350g
Average wingspan	96cms	92cms
Average length	38.5cms	37cms

Food: Around 80 per cent of food is made up of field voles. Also young rats, small birds, beetles.

UK range: Breeding range extensive apart from southern England and Wales. Widespread dispersal in winter.

World distribution: North and South America, Europe and northern Asia.

Breeding: Nests on the ground in the shelter of tall grass or heather. Breeding activity starts in mid-April. Eggs laid in unlined scrape, normally 4 to 8, but 14 have been known when food is plentiful. Eggs laid at 2-day intervals. Incubation period around 26 days, beginning with the first egg. Young leave the nest at about 2 weeks old but cannot fly for another 10 days.

From the beginner's point of view, this bird's name is very misleading because the ear tufts are so short and hidden that they are almost invisible. The short-eared owl is the closest living relative to the long-eared, but its habitat could not be more different.

Shorties are **birds of open spaces**; they live and hunt on moorlands, marshes and sand dunes. With unusually long wings for owls,

In common with many small species, this little owl has false eye patches on its back to deter predators from attacking

space to glide and soar long distances without being troubled by such matters. And, unlike long-eareds, short-eareds are a **daylight species**, hence their old name 'day owl'. Their hearing is only a little better than a crow's and the physical design of their eyes suggests that their sight has evolved to work better in bright light rather than darkness. They spend their nights roosting either on the ground or in low bushes, and instead of the typical upright owl posture, these birds rest horizontally; they stand on their legs but look as if they are lying down on their chest.

Compared with moorland, a wood is a complicated ecosystem that supports literally hundreds of animal species. The bilberry and heather-clad upland home of the short-eared owl is a much more specialised environment with far fewer animals. To survive, shorties depend almost entirely on the population level of field voles, and this fluctuates wildly from year to year. These small rodents can form up to 80 per cent of the owl's diet; when numbers are high, the owls do well, but if the voles are hard to find, the owls are forced by near-starvation to move away.

Shorties are great wanderers. Their movements, however, do not follow any logical pattern and they travel almost randomly looking for food, particularly in winter when the high moors are snowbound and inhospitable. They are one of the **most migratory of all owls** and might nest in a different place each year, ending up hundreds – if not thousands

they are well adapted for an existence in an open landscape. Woodland species have a shorter wingspan that gives them the ability to dodge around trees. Shorties have the

– of kilometres away from where they hatched.

Should they find a good hunting spot with plenty of voles, the owls can gather in high numbers, forgetting their mutual dislike of each other to concentrate on eating. In really bad conditions owls from the Continent move over to Britain, while at the same time our resident shorties move to the very south of the country.

Like so many others, these owls are partial to airfields in winter, for these are one of the few places that are kept clear of snow, no matter how thick or persistent it might be. The huge clearing machines suck up the snow and blow it away from the path of aircraft, leaving thin strips of open grassland on the edge of runways. This might be the only exposed vegetation around and will inevitably attract mammals and small birds to feed.

Both of these make ideal targets for hungry short-eared owls and anyone who carefully watches a northern airport in winter has a good chance of seeing these birds floating around and dropping silently on to the grass. Sadly for all concerned, though, the harmless hunting owls are a real threat to aircraft. As they fly over the runways the birds sometimes get caught in the air intakes of jet engines, causing the motor to stall, which ´either results in an expensive repair bill or, even worse, an accident. Whatever happens to the aircraft, the outcome of an airstrike for the unfortunate owl is always instant death. It is difficult to see how this can be avoided, but short-eared owls face another lethal problem that can certainly be prevented. Each year an unknown number are killed by unscrupulous or careless hunters. Short-eared owls share many moorlands with grouse and all too often they are shot when beaters drive birds of all species into the path of the guns. Identification comes only when the dogs pick up the corpse of an owl instead of a grouse.

At home on wild northern moors where shooting is forbidden, short-eared owls lead a less hazardous life. But even here they are not completely safe. When territories overlap, shorties might be killed and eaten by the bigger and more powerful **snowy owls**. Even if the snowies do not actually catch them, they will indulge in robbery with violence by chasing and dive-bombing the shorties when they are carrying prey, forcing them to drop the food to protect themselves. Snowy owls have learned that it is easier to intimidate smaller owls into giving up their food than it is to catch prey for themselves. In addition, some crows, one of the world's most intelligent birds, are expert at terrorising the owls and making them give up their prey.

Yet short-eared owls are not defenceless and can be aggressive, especially during the breeding season. On days in early spring, when territorial wars are still being waged, paired birds will work together to drive out intruders. Because of its diurnal life style, this is one of the few species that have **visual displays**. When males are trying to attract mates, they produce probably the most exciting aerobatics in the owl world. They start off with a solo flight up to about 500 metres above the ground, sometimes singing in low, rapid hoots. At the highest point, where no female could possibly miss his tricks, the male goes through a series of shallow dives, each ending in an upward swoop, clapping his wings loudly together on the downbeat. He finishes with a dramatic lunge towards the ground, which looks as if it will end in a suicidal crash, before pulling out at the last possible moment. He keeps up this flamboyant display until a female shows interest.

Once the pair-bond has been made, the eggs are laid in a **scrape** on the ground and incubated by the female. If the site is disturbed the male is likely to attack the interloper, although determined foxes and crows often manage to get through and steal the eggs. Ground-nesters are always more at risk and the young have an instinctive strategy of behaviour to safeguard themselves from the extra dangers that do not face tree-nesting owls. Instead of the usual loud screeching and begging that greets the arrival of food in other species, short-eared chicks are very restrained in their calling to avoid giving away their location. Youngsters also usually leave the nest-site long before they can fend for themselves. They separate and can distance themselves up to 200 metres from the nest, which again is a safety precaution, for should an enemy appear it will probably find just one or two of them instead of the whole brood. Having left the nest, the chicks attract their parents' attention by lying flat and shaking their wings. Food is dropped and the adult leaves without drawing attention to its vulnerable young.

Short-eared owls are in no great danger in Britain since food is plentiful and their breeding moorlands are not wanted as building-sites. But as farming techniques improve, it is possible that more of the habitat will be cultivated. Then the owls will really suffer.

Snowy owl (*Nyctea scandiaca*)

	Female	Male
Average weight	2.3kg	1.8kg
Average wingspan	1.52m	1.4m
Average length	62.5cm	58.5cm

Food: In Britain they feed on rabbits, mice and birds.

UK range: Northern Scottish islands and occasional visitor to Scottish mainland.

World distribution: Greenland, northern Canada, northern Scandinavia, northern Russia and Siberia.

Breeding: Nests on the ground, may be lined with moss, feathers, etc. Activity starts in late April. Number of eggs can range from 3 to 10, depending on food availability. 14 eggs have

Snowy owl

been known. Incubation begins with first egg and lasts around 35 days. Young leave the nest around 5 or 6 weeks old but cannot fly well for another 3 weeks.

There are people who believe that snowy owls do not belong on a list of resident British birds, because their numbers are so low and their recent breeding record has been non-existent. Snowy owls are a **sub-arctic species**, at home in the cold wilderness areas of Canada, Scandinavia and Russia. In colder times they lived much further south in central Europe, but as the climate slowly warmed, the owls followed the snowline north.

Snowies were almost certainly a breeding bird in Britain in ages past and there were unproved rumours of snowy owls rearing young on the Shetland Islands twice during the nineteenth century. They are one of the biggest owls in the world and breed freely in Norway, just 500 kilometres from the north-eastern islands of Scotland – a relatively small trip for such a large bird. There have been dozens of confirmed sightings of vagrant snowy owls that stayed for a time and then disappeared, presumably back to their home-land. But the first authenticated instance of chicks hatching in Britain was recorded on the small island of Fetlar in 1967. Males had been seen here for the previous four years, but there were no females to pair with. That year a party of birdwatchers saw a male perching on a rock and, instead of flying away, he flew towards them giving a threat display. This meant there had to be a female nearby and a bond had already formed.

The event took the British ornithological world by storm. It was one of the most exciting events to have happened in decades. Once the male and female snowy owls had taken up territory and laid seven eggs, the Royal Society for the Protection of Birds immediately set up a twenty-four-hour warden watch to protect the unique pair from the well-meaning but often over-enthusiastic birdwatchers that flocked north to see the VIP arrivals. Egg-collectors were an even more sinister danger. Although the snowies were fully protected by law, it was well known that their blown eggs would be an irresistible prize for unscrupulous oologists keen to add a first to their collection.

The wardens' vigil paid off when six young birds hatched on a British island for the first time in recorded history (the seventh egg was infertile). Their progress and behaviour were intimately watched, timed, studied and analysed, the chicks became headline news on television and in the papers. The Shetland snowies were probably the most well-documented owls in the world. There were many moments of concern, but the most dramatic came when a young snowy flew into a barbed-wire fence and cut its wing badly. However, after medical attention that involved twenty-three stitches, the bird soon recovered.

The same pair nested on Fetlar until 1974, when the male disappeared, leaving only female birds. There was – and still is – a debate about the possibility of releasing more snowy owls into the Shetlands. They breed prolifically in captivity and, carefully introduced, a group of unrelated chicks would probably settle down to nest, re-establishing the snowy owl as a resident species.

Yet there is a strong argument against such a release scheme. Snowies belong in the far north; on Fetlar they were at about the most southerly point of their breeding range. The fact that they nested at all could simply have been the result of two adult birds being in the same place by accident. The striking arctic coloration is out of place in the relatively mild climate of Fetlar. Being so obvious, the snowies were always being mobbed by flocks of hooded crows.

These owls are built for life in the cold tundra and can tolerate extremes of temperature that would kill other species. Although they are not closely related, snowies occupy a similar position in their own habitat to that of **eagle owls** in theirs. They even have ear tufts, which are so small that they are rarely seen. The **male owl** is **pure white** and his **mate** is **flecked with chocolate brown** to make her less visible when sitting on eggs. The colour is partly for camouflage in frost and snow but it also helps to keep the birds warm, as less heat is lost from a white surface than from any other colour. Their legs and feet are protected from the biting cold by a dense layer of feathers that almost covers their strong, curved talons. These owls also have an eccentric 'moustached' appearance, created by the long feathers around their beaks.

Biologically there is no reason why snowy owls should not live and breed in Britain, although the first pair had to modify their diet slightly to fit the new habitat. In Canada and Europe, snowies feed heavily on lemmings, but these animals do not exist in the Shetlands. Rabbits, however, offer an excellent alternative, supplemented with oystercatchers, skuas and any other bird that comes too near.

Snowy owls are mainly **diurnal** and while they lack the equipment for silent flight, they are fast and powerful in the air. Although considerably smaller than his mate, the male is a very aggressive creature. From a high vantage point close to the nest, he sits and watches for anything that threatens his family. He will attack humans, sheep and even ponies that get too close, either by an aerial bombardment or by running directly towards the trespasser in a low, hunch-backed crouch. Rival males will fight in the air, lashing out with talons that often lock together so that both birds lose control and spin towards the earth before they release. Direct battle is avoided by using hoots: the deep, low call of the male travels up to a mile in the unbroken solitude of the arctic tundra. As fewer animals live in the far north, snowy owls have a very large territory. There may not have been any rivals to warn, but the Fetlar male bravely used his voice to declare that his patch was out of bounds.

When times are good the male will catch more prey than he needs to feed his family; which is stored in a cache not far from the nest. The free supply of pre-killed food

Two young snowy owls

attracts scavengers, but they are viciously driven off and might even be added to the pantry if they are not swift enough to avoid the male snowy's fatal grip.

At two weeks old the young leave the nest and hide, while the female broods younger siblings. All of the youngsters, however, are fed for some weeks after leaving. Once they become fully independent, young snowy owls might travel vast distances before taking possession of a territory.

The future of snowy owls in Britain is simply a matter of guesswork, even for experts. It is likely, though, that they will continue to be occasional visitors that breed here only when conditions are right.

Barn owl (*Tyto alba*)

	Female	Male
Average weight	375g	320g
Average wingspan	76cm	74cm
Average length	35cm	33cm

Food: Small mammals make up 95 per cent of the diet, mainly voles. Also eat insects, frogs and lizards.

UK range: Covers most of the mainland of Britain and Ireland. Generally avoids built-up areas and high ground.

World distribution: North and South America, western Europe, much of Africa, southern Asia, and Australia.

Breeding: Nests in old buildings, working barns and even churches. Also hollow trees, caves and nest boxes. Average 6 eggs, 15 have been known. Eggs laid at 1-2 day- intervals, incubation begins with first. Incubation period lasts around 35 days.Chicks first fly at about 60 days old and are completely independent at ten weeks.

In many people's eyes barn owls are *the* true owls – the classic bird of nocturnal farmyards, silent and mysterious, but still familiar and welcome. With their bright plumage and heart-shaped face (ornithologists with a less-romantic turn of phrase have named them the 'monkey-faced owls') barn owls are the most distinctive members of the family. In the past decade, millions of words have been written about the plight of barn owls in Britain. Most popular newspapers and magazines have jumped on the bandwagon at some stage to voice their outrage at the impending demise of the species. Like countless other observers, I can't help thinking that perhaps the objections would not be quite so widespread and loud if the barn owl was less attractive and 'cuddly'.

To put the record straight and give a fairer view of the problem, it needs to be looked at in a global perspective. Barn owls are possibly the most widely distributed of *any* bird species; they have been described, with some justification, as the most successful bird on earth. Barn owls can be found in North and

South America, Europe, Asia, Africa and Australia. In most places their populations are either stable or increasing. Throughout the tropical belt, barn owls are prolific breeders, often raising two broods in a season. The difficulties facing British barn owls are a local problem which, as far as the overall welfare of the species is concerned, has little bearing on the long-term future.

But that is the objective, logical view. Speaking more personally, the loss of barn owls from the British landscape would be a disaster. And that is a real possibility. At the moment there are an estimated 4500 breeding pairs, a tiny number considering the size of the country. It hasn't always been like this – fossil remains even show that barn owls were present before man. In those days they would have nested in caves and hollow trees, sites they still use today when buildings are not available. Exact figures are elusive but we do know that from the late eighteenth century their numbers grew rapidly. A series of Enclosures Acts forced landowners to mark and protect their fields, giving up the open-farming strip system where boundaries were just narrow belts of grass. This political move radically changed much of the countryside and introduced the wide spread use of hedgerows, a vitally important hunting ground for barn owls.

At about the same time the human population was going through a minor boom. To feed the extra mouths, more land was cultivated and cereal crops grown. The well stocked fields provided food for small rodents, and their numbers multiplied as they bred in the shelter of newly created hedges. The barn owls were suddenly presented with an increased food supply. Grain collection and storage was primitive in those days; much was dropped during harvesting and in the farmyards it was not kept inside round steel silos that we use now, but in wooden sheds that are no barrier to mice and rats. Farm buildings were over-run with rodents, and the owls followed them. Reports of mice plagues came in from all parts of the country, with tales of farmers who could uncover thousands simply by moving a few bales of straw. In the first quarter of the nineteenth century the population of barn owls was probably at its highest level in history. It was possibly the most common owl in Britain and a familiar sight to all countrymen. The renowned eighteenth century naturalist Comte de Buffon (1707-1788) said barn owls were numerous throughout Europe, but nowhere more so than in Britain.

This utopian state did not last long, for it was the nineteenth century that saw the growth of the hunting estate. This was land set aside and managed for sportsmen who would pay for the privilege of shooting birds. Pheasants and partridges were reared in huge numbers to provide sport for the users of newly-invented, mass-produced guns. To ensure that the maximum number of birds

could be taken, gamekeepers were employed to destroy predators that might kill the birds before the lead pellets could. Any creature that included, or was even rumoured to include, game birds in its diet became a legitimate target. In some places carnivores were almost completely wiped out. The invention of a pole-trap, a particularly nasty device for catching birds, and the breech-loading gun gave humans a destructive ability that went wildly out of control. Birds of prey, stoats, weasels, magpies, wild cats and every other species were slaughtered in their millions – along with owls.

Barn owls were a particularly easy target compared with other species because of their semi-diurnal habits and bright colours. Their proximity to man made them even more vulnerable; they regularly nested in buildings just a minute's walk from the houses of keepers employed to kill them. In counties where shooting estates were large and powerful, barn owls were almost wiped out in less than thirty years. The ironic point is that as the larger hunters were slowly wiped out, the number of rats increased because their predators were disappearing. The army of rats was responsible for the death of far more game birds than ever could have been caused by the birds of prey and other carnivores that were steadily being killed.

A barn owl, whose long legs can only really be seen when they are in flight

Unfortunately, all of this coincided with the development of a morbid interest in egg-collecting and taxidermy. Barn owl trophies were highly sought after by socially aware Victorians. Owls in their thousands were shot, stuffed and artistically displayed in glass cases. Most were shown holding a blood-stained mouse but some (and I quote from a catalogue list) 'show the heart-warming scene of a mother owl protecting her three young babies'. There were some far-sighted conservationists that warned of the consequences if this continued but they were ignored and the owl's plight became increasingly desperate. In the second half of the nineteenth century there was a succession of extremely hard winters – as barn owls suffer terribly in cold, snowy conditions it seemed that even the weather gods were against them. There was a brief recovery at the beginning of this century, brought about by a combination of milder winters and the onset of World War I, which took countless keepers of the land and away from their traps.

It was only a temporary respite and the owl's long term outlook was looking increasingly bleak even at that time. The countryside was becoming ever more tidy and orderly; there was less wastage of cereal grain as mechanisation took over. Hedges and copses were pulled out to make way for bigger fields that were more practical for tractors. In the south, barn owls went into decline that has never been reversed and has since spread to

Barn owl chick at two weeks old

all parts of Britain. A 1932 survey, that was not complete but innovative for its day, suggested that around 12,000 breeding pairs still survived – a figure that is almost three times higher than levels today.

The number of barn owls has always fluctuated, as does the population of most species. The success of British barn owls is closely tied in with that of **field voles**, their main prey. As the number of rodents' varies, so does the number of barn owls. These owls are also at the mercy of the weather: they are a **lowland species** and 80 per cent breed at an altitude of less than 125 metres above sea-level. Here they are sheltered from the worst of the winter conditions. Snow poses probably the greatest natural risk to these slight owls because, when it lies, their prey stays at ground level beneath the white blanket and the owls simply cannot reach it. Active barn owls have low fat reserves – around 5 per cent of their body weight – and after a few days without a thaw this store is used up and the owls start to die of starvation.

Late snowfalls, in March or April, can be catastrophic in other ways. The male must find food to give to his prospective mate to initiate courtship. He sometimes collects extra food at the chosen nest-site to impress the female with his hunting prowess, which is a good strategy, as she will look for a partner that has proved himself to be a hunter that can supply enough prey for both her and her chicks. The female needs to increase her body weight before laying – sometimes as much as 25 per cent – to see her through the incubation period. Without sufficient food there may be no successful pairing that year and many birds only experience one chance to nest because of their relatively low life-expectancy. On the other hand, mild winters give the rodents a longer breeding season, and their increased numbers encourage owls to start nesting earlier and to produce bigger clutches.

Female barn owls make attentive and gentle parents. Towards the end of the incubation period, as the eggs are due to hatch, the female sits motionless and listens to them. Twenty-four hours before they are due to emerge, the chicks inside begin to call quietly, and the female then knows that hatching is about to begin. Once the chick has made the first crack in the egg, the female delicately picks off small pieces of shell to assist her helpless offspring. The process takes a long time as the chicks soon become exhausted and have to rest. Once it is free, the female cleans the chick's soft down by nibbling with her beak. If the male appears at this sensitive stage, he is likely to be driven away immediately by his highly protective mate.

The best place to look for barn owls is **mixed farmland**, with small hedged fields and the odd wood. They like to hunt over unmown grasslands and are very partial to riverbanks that have not been cleared of vegetation. **White owls**, as they are often called, can regularly be seen hunting in daylight, particularly in spring, when they have to find food for a growing family, or in winter, when prey is hard to find at any time of the day or night.

For centuries, barn owls have been involved with man. Two-thirds **nest in buildings** and much of their finest hunting habitat was created by early farming practices. When crops were cut and gathered by hand, it was a slow laborious task. Once the corn was cut it was dried in stooks, often staying like that for several weeks, which gave small animals the opportunity to eat their fill and even carry away food to store in an underground larder, but the development and speed of modern farming practices has put an end to this.

Harvested grain is now kept in strong metal silos, making farmyards far less attractive feeding grounds for rodents and, consequently, their predators. With their quick and effective packing of crops, combine harvesters clear the fields in a single day, with little waste. To make way for the giant machine, fields were made bigger by ripping out hedges and woods. The importance of this last action cannot be over-emphasised – one research project showed that barn owls catch 95 per cent of their food on the edge of a woodland.

Hay fields, one of the best hunting grounds, are also gradually disappearing. With the perfection of man-made, concentrated foodstuffs that can be fed to animals during the winter, hay has become less important and grass fields have been turned over to different crops. Throughout much of the country, Dutch elm disease completely wiped out a very important nesting tree, and barn owls were not even able to make use of the tree remains, as conscientious landowners rightly burned the dead trees to reduce the chance of the disease spreading further.

In recent years there has been a trend for people to move out of cities and back into the countryside, and they all need somewhere to live. Almost overnight the tasteful barn-conversion became an expensive and sought-after status symbol. The traditional homes of thousands of barn owls were turned into desirable residences – for humans. Farm buildings themselves have changed, too. Gone are the sturdy, brick-built barns with windowsills, storage ledges and other nooks and crannies. Huge wall-less Dutch barns were introduced, which are cold draughty places that provide little in the way of a nest-site. In the 1950s the ultimate horror was introduced – chemical sprays (see chapter 9) which wreaked havoc on the already battered owl population.

At this stage I would like to say that farmers and landowners should not be seen as the unfeeling ogres of the barn owl saga. They have the same commercial pressures as every other businessman. Moreover, like all human activities, our approach to food production constantly alters with new knowledge and inventions. Without these advances the world simply could not survive. Some animals have benefited from the modifications; others, like the barn owl, have not been so fortunate. Two hundred years ago their numbers increased because of changes in the way land was used; today their numbers are dropping, for exactly the same reason.

The plight of the barn owl has been written about often and, as a result, the bird has become a household name. Yet they are still often confused with other species. Barn owls are smaller than tawnies but, at night, with their white underwings showing against the black sky, they look much larger than they really are. I have had countless disputes with people who claim that they have seen 'snowy owls' hunting in a field behind their house.

Barn owls do look very big at night (and much smaller in daylight), particularly if they appear without warning. It is a simple optical illusion brought about by the pure white plumage on the owl's underside showing against the blackness. The angle of view also causes problems, as from below it is only possible to see the white feathers that cover the chest and underwings. The beautiful fawn, grey and silver feathers of the bird's back and head are hidden.

The barn owl's colour has perplexed experts for years. If anyone was to be given the job of designing, from scratch, a nocturnal bird predator that specialised in catching mice and small mammals on the ground, it is highly likely that dark brown would be chosen as the basic colour. Black owls are few and far between, which indicates that black is probably not the best overall colour; it might be most suitable for hunting purposes but, through evolutionary experimentation, most species have adopted dark brown, with mottled patches of black and grey to hide them when hunting and give camouflage during the day. Barn owls defy convention – or common sense – and no one quite knows why.

Certainly, its light feathers help to hide the bird when it hunts in daylight, but as these owls are mainly nocturnal, this creates more problems than it solves. There is a theory that the barn owl's light plumage is a way of signalling visually to other members of the species, warning them that this territory is taken. Barn owls are generally silent and do not use sound to proclaim tenancy, so sight needs to play a greater part in communication. But this idea has one obvious flaw: if barn owls are visible to each other from a distance, they will also be visible to their potential prey.

Colour can be of some help when sexing barn owls; although females are larger than males, there is not much difference in dimensions. Generally males have lighter back feathers and fewer black flecks on their chest. But this can be misleading because females become lighter with age, until they are almost indistinguishable from males. This, along with the fact that there is a lot of variation between individuals, makes colour sexing a guide that is not altogether reliable.

8 A World Full of Owls

According to the most widely accepted list, there are 133 species of owl in the world, although there other schools of thought that have numbers ranging from 121 to 142 species. The exact figure depends on how the subspecies are counted. These are birds distinguished from the main population by differences in physical characteristics, such as size or plumage. The species list keeps changing in subtle ways and probably always will as new facts are unearthed that fill the gaps in our knowledge.

Owl species throughout the world have a great deal in common, no matter what habitat they occupy. They can be found in huge numbers on every continent apart from Antarctica. This shows the adaptability of the entire family and illustrates just how well designed they are for the job of survival. Owls are always portrayed as being totally nocturnal but only 80 of the world's species are truly hunters of the night.

Although they all share a standard body shape, owls come in a range of sizes. The biggest species, the **eagle owl**, is almost one hundred times heavier than the smallest, the **elf owl** of southern USA and Mexico.

This tiny bird is only fractionally bigger than a sparrow and lives on a diet of locusts, grasshoppers and other insects. Catching creatures as small as this does not require great strength or powerful weapons; relative to their size, elf owls have unusually weak beaks and claws.

The elf owl's armoury is very different from that of the **ferruginous pygmy owl** from central and south America. They have strong beaks and talons which are capable of catching house sparrows, a bird that is almost as big as the owl itself; most of their food consists of insects, including scorpions. Ferruginous pygmy owls are daytime hunters that do not object to the presence of humans. In many suburbs they perch, unnoticed, on overhead wires while searching for food. Their tiny size and fast, jerky flight makes

The eagle owl is the largest of all species

them look more like small garden birds rather than owls.

This is in sharp contrast to a species that may live close by, the **great horned owl**. These have the reputation of being one of the most ferocious and aggressive birds in the world; Americans call them the 'flying tigers'. I know one ornithologist, visiting a farm in California, who watched in fascination as a great horned made three attempts to catch the local tomcat. This was a big, battle scarred animal that was suitably terrified of the deadly owl and only just managed to escape when the farmer opened a door and frightened off the hungry bird.

Great horned owls will not tolerate the presence of any other owl inside their territory and intruders are usually killed immediately. While the other owls will take up residence in abandoned nests, the great horned does not always wait until the original owners have left. They are very partial to the flat platforms built by red-tailed hawks and once a suitable nest has been finished by a pair of these industrious birds, the owls move in and drive them away. The 'flying tigers' have an instant nursery that needs no work, while the hawks are forced to start all over again. Great horned owls are at the top of the food chain and a healthy adult has no real enemies, although youngsters are sometimes taken by agile black bears that climb trees to reach the nest.

Since I first became interested in owls, I have watched them in many different habitats, but the individual that stands out most in my memory was a member of a little-known and small species of American owl called the saw-whet. We came across it on Amhurst Island in Canada, where we met an amiable local birdwatcher who told us that he had seen a saw-whet just that morning. He gave us precise directions to a plantation in the middle of the island and added confidently: 'The owl was sitting in a red cedar tree.' We carefully followed the instructions, walked and skidded over a frozen field, jumped across a small stream and stopped in our tracks. In front was a sea of red cedars, thousands of them. Our guide had neglected to say in which tree he had seen the owl.

We separated. Keith Offord took the left side of the forest and I took the right. Most roosting owls like to sit close to the main trunk of a tree, which makes them impossible to spot from the outside if they have chosen to sleep in a conifer. We had to separate the lower branches of *each cedar* to look for an owl that is about the size of a blackbird. After two hours of fruitless searching, tree-examination became automatic. Open the branches, quick look round, no owl, move on. I have no idea how many cedars I looked into that morning.

I was getting close to the point of never wanting to see another red cedar ever again, when I parted two branches and there, with-

The engaging, elusive saw-whet owl

in touching distance, was a roosting saw-whet. Its feathers were fluffed out to ward off the ice-cold wind and, at the sound of my sudden appearance, its eyelids opened slightly to reveal a pair of golden-brown eyes. Saw-whets roost on much lower branches than other owls and it was only a little way above my head. I froze completely, waiting for the owl to explode into action and fly off into the shelter of the thick forest. It did nothing. I reached into my bag for a camera and lens and, as quietly as possible and, without breathing, I photographed the owl. This was a new species for me, so I went through an entire roll of film in a matter of minutes. And still the owl did not move. I photographed it with close-up lenses, wide-angle and telephoto lenses . . . the bird did not budge. It watched me lazily for the first fifteen minutes and then went back to sleep. At one stage my head was no more than ten centimetres from it, yet it remained aloof and unconcerned.

I had never seen any bird behave this way before – I've photographed seabirds on remote islands that were almost as tame, but at least they stayed awake to watch the proceedings. This saw-whet was simply not interested in me. I spent over an hour taking photographs during which time it did not move once. When photographing any wild animal, it is good to capture a lively expression. With most species that is automatic as they have an idea that a human is nearby and are already watchful and alert. If the animal is very laid-back, it can be woken up with a soft sound made by a low whistle or tapping two small stones together. I tried both with dismal results, I doubt if I could have stirred this owl with a starting pistol. It was the most co-operative wild animal I have ever encountered.

Saw-whets are one of the least documented of America's owls and there are areas of their life history that are a complete blank to scientists. But everyone agrees that these small birds are tame to an extent that is hard to believe. There are reports of people picking them up, closely examining them and then putting them back on to the perch. The owls then promptly go back to sleep.

Local knowledge is the best way to find owls but sometimes it can prove to be a problem. On a trip to the Gambia in West Africa, I went off in search of a **white-faced scops owl,** as there is a famous roost on the edge of a golf course where an owl can be seen on most days. It took only a few minutes to spot the sleepy bird sitting high in a tree and there it quietly stayed as I took photographs with a telephoto lens.

Suddenly a young Gambian lad appeared and told me that the owl 'belonged to the golf course' and, if I wanted to take photographs, I would have to pay for the privilege. I asked why, since it was a wild owl and did not belong to anyone, there should be a charge. He thought about this for a while and then replied, 'We need the money to buy food for the owl.' It was a good try but as the white-

said about the majority of the world's owls. Some are so rare and secretive that virtually nothing is known about their habits. The **stygian owl**, mysterious in both looks and name, is a close relative of the long-eared, but all we know about these birds is that they live in the forests of central and South America. Hardly anything is known about their food, behaviour or breeding habits.

Dense woodlands can hinder any kind of serious owl study. In West Africa there is an evasive and shy species called the **vermiculated fishing owl**, which lives in the mature woodlands alongside wide rivers. Most experts think that these birds are rare, but this could simply reflect the lack of thorough research rather than a lack of owls.

In 1969 a vermiculated fishing owl was found on the deck of a cargo boat that had just left the West African coast en route, non-stop, to Liverpool. On its arrival in England on 29 October the bird was presented to Chester Zoo where, at the time of writing, it still lives happily. Chester has an excellent collection of owls and one of the finest breeding records in Europe. With so many natural habitats under direct threat, the future of highly endangered species might lie in intelligent, well-managed captive breeding projects. Run properly, zoos and private collections should have an important role to play in the conservation of rare animals. While some zoos, in my opinion, leave much to be desired, others do invaluable work in fields

Vermiculated fishing owl

faced scops exists by catching live insects, his story was less than convincing.

There are sixteen recorded species of scops owl and they are closely related to the twelve known screech owls. More than half of the scops species are under real threat and, as many of them live on islands where space is limited, their future does not look rosy.

The white-faced scops owl in Gambia was very approachable, but the same cannot be

such as genetics and behaviour. Most will 'loan' animals to other reputable collections on a long-term basis in order to establish breeding pairs. Money is rarely an issue as these projects are genuine attempts to prevent extinction. Zoos often become world renowned for encouraging the breeding of just a few species; this adds to our knowledge of the animals and gives them a better chance of survival. The ultimate aim is to release captive-bred birds back into their natural environment.

Fishing owls are a curious bunch: catching and eating fish seems such a very un-owl-like thing to do. These birds are the nocturnal counterparts of ospreys and are just as accomplished at flying low over a river and snatching prey directly out of the water. Fishing owls have long, sharp talons, that act just like an angler's hook, and the fleshy underpart of the toes is covered with rough skin to help them hold on to wriggling, slippery fish. Fishing owls are large – some are almost the size of eagle owls – and are totally nocturnal.

Most owls have, on every continent, an equivalent species which is a similar size, eats the same kind of food and occupies a parallel habitat. Woodlands of Britain are home to the tawny owl, while in North America they give shelter to the related **barred owl**. Just like tawnies, barred owls are vocal, noisy creatures that ward off rivals with a wide range of loud vibrating calls. If anything, barred owls have an even greater vocal repertoire than their European cousins and their shrieks can only be described as demonic, sounding more like the squalling of argumentative cats than birds.

The similar African nocturnal niche is occupied by the dark-eyed, dark-feathered **wood owl**, which lives mainly inside dense forests. However, a few have been seen recently in the leafier suburbs of Cape Town, as these birds gradually become urbanised, just like the European tawny.

The barn owl is represented in Africa by a dark-breasted subspecies that behaves in much the same way as the European form. Local farmers are fully aware of the value of having these birds around for their rodent-catching skills, and they will go to considerable lengths to encourage them. **African barn owls** rear their young in old buildings and hollow trees, but they are also very keen on moving into the large, deserted nests of hammerkops. These are odd-looking wading birds that build spherical nests out of twigs, with an entrance hole that is just the right diameter for a barn owl. Although European and African barn owls look quite different, the two can breed together to produce fertile young.

Giant owls can be found on most continents. In Europe we have the 'great' eagle owls and there are several species in Africa.

American barred owls are slightly larger than the European tawny

Hawk owl in nest box

The **spotted eagle owl** is the smallest member of the family. It can be seen hunting along grassy verges on major highways and muddy tracks throughout southern Africa, but sadly many suffer the same fate as countless owls that fly too close to traffic. Although this bird is nowhere near as large as its cousin the European eagle owl, it is a good size yet, surprisingly, it lives mainly on insects. Spotted eagle owls will catch mice, lizards and other small animals, but the bulk of their diet is made up of enormous numbers of creepy-crawlies.

This is a very different menu from that enjoyed by their neighbours, the **milky eagle owls**, known locally as **giant eagle owls**. These voracious creatures eat guinea fowl, hares and even the occasional genet (a large cat-like animal). The curious thing about milky eagle owls is that they have very pale upper eyelids. When they blink, there is a brief flash of white as the eyelids open and close. This is probably used to communicate with other sharp-eyed owls on even the darkest night.

Australia has an impressive species known as the **powerful owl**, which is the largest member of the **hawk owl** group. It is relatively uncommon and can only be found in some forests in the southeast. Much more widely distributed is its smaller cousin, the **boobook owl**, which also lives in New Zealand and New Guinea. The majority of Australians know this as the **morepork**, pronounced 'mo-poke', a name that mimics the bird's call. The boobook is a lean, swift bird that lives mainly on insects, although it will catch reptiles and small mammals when the opportunity arises. In New Zealand the boobook has direct competition for food and breeding grounds from a tough and aggressive newcomer that was introduced earlier this century, the **little owl**.

9 Owls and Man

The earliest-known reference to owls is a sculpture that dates back to the last Ice Age and can be seen in a cave at Trois Frères, France. The scene shows snowy owls with chicks, and was carved at a time when the great glaciers had made their way deep into Europe, bringing with them arctic wildlife. Remains of charred and smashed bones indicate that early man was interested in snowy owls not only as models but as food.

The history of the relationship between owls and man is very varied. For thousands of years the two existed alongside each other without event, treating each other with a mutual, healthy respect. As man became more powerful and destructive, however, the balance shifted, with the owls, among other creatures, as losers.

Farming

Once man began to change the landscape by cutting down forests and planting crops, he altered the whole ecosystem of his habitat. At first this would have been in small, unimportant ways – the population of Stone Age people in Britain probably never exceeded a few thousand, which was a tiny, inconsequential number in a countryside that was still wild and home to wolves, bears and lynx. Man would have caused some deforestation and hunted a few animals but not on a large enough scale to make a major difference. As weapons and tools became more advanced, humans ate better, they could build more secure homes and defend themselves against wild animals. Their life span increased and numbers slowly grew, along with their influence on the countryside around. The expanding population meant a need for more houses, food and animal skins for clothes.

When the first Agricultural Revolution began, nothing in the natural world would ever be quite the same again. In a relatively short time we changed from a semi-nomadic species, which survived by hunting meat and gathering seasonal fruit and nuts, to an organised, settled society that planned for the

Tawny owl

Barn owls in one of their favourite habitats

future by planting crops that would be stored to provide food throughout the year. Instead of merely taking advantage of our environment, humans began to control and alter it.

In some ways this was beneficial to wildlife, including owls. The massive increase of cereal crops gave small mammals an endless food supply, which, in turn, eventually provided food for the owls. But to make room for fields and settlements, the huge areas of woodland that once carpeted much of Europe were slowly but steadily cut down. Even in prehistoric times, forest animals were losing ground to the relentless push of civilisation. Later, habitat destruction was almost a way of life in the Middle Ages, with millions of trees being felled to make the half-timbered houses that are so much admired and sought after today. The expanding British navy needed vast quantities of timber to make the ships that first navigated many of the world's unknown oceans. This was truly a time of innovation, exploration and destruction.

Some of our actions were accidentally good for the owl population. During his trade with far and exotic lands, man has introduced several new species into Britain. House mice and black and brown rats were carried here in the form of stowaways on board ships; rabbits were intentionally imported as food by the Norman invaders in the eleventh century. All of these tough little mammals readily adapted to their new home and quickly colonised the whole country. Suddenly the resident predators were presented with a nonstop source of food. But the reverse also happened; whenever settlers moved into strange new colonies, they often wanted to take along reminders of home. On countless voyages around the globe, wild animals were packed away in small cages for release when the new homeland was reached. Sadly (but ecologically fortunately) most died shortly after arrival, unable to adjust to the strange surroundings, food and predators.

Some did make the transition and learned to survive, often to the detriment of the existing wildlife. African **grass owls**, a close relative of the barn owl, were introduced into the Seychelle Islands to help combat the rats that infested the commercial coconut plantations. The only resident owl, the **Seychelles owl**, was not big enough to handle rats – grass owls could. At least that was the theory, but the owls had different ideas. Instead of catching rats, the grass owls chose to hunt local birds, species that were unique to the Seychelles and often already highly endangered. The rats continued to thrive and prosper while the immigrant owls slowly ate their way through some of the world's rarest birds.

The Seychelles owl could not compete with these powerful newcomers. Before the introduction project began it was a rare species; faced with grass owls, the Seychelles owl went on to become one of the most threatened on earth. Today there is an attempt to rid the islands of grass owls but it may not be finished in time to save the birds that are barely hanging on to survival.

Long before the Seychelles experiment, farmers throughout Europe realised that owls were a valuable ally in the control of the pests that destroyed their crops. Most new barns incorporated round holes close to the top of the roof, leading to a small attic where 'white owls' could nest. It has taken modern landowners a long time to realise that these early farmers knew exactly what they were doing, as this form of biological control is cheap, effective and environmentally friendly. In the tropics, many fruit plantations are plagued by rats which cost millions of pounds in eaten or contaminated crops. Wise managers have installed strong, weatherproof nest boxes for barn owls, and have seen a dramatic drop in the number of rats as these skilful, self-perpetuating, low-maintenance rodent operatives silently glide through the plantations in search of food for themselves and their chicks.

Some of the side effects of farming have helped owls in very obscure ways. The introduction and domestication of grazing animals such as sheep has, over many centuries, produced a new kind of habitat, grassland. Wide expanses of grass would have been very rare, if not unknown, in early Britain, but the need to feed man's flocks changed that. Established hay meadows became one of the best hunting grounds for barn owls, and little owls, too, are very partial to closely grazed grass, where they can hunt for creepy-crawlies. But what we give, we can also take away. In the last eighty years some places have lost 95 per cent of their old meadows, depriving birds of prey of a larder and ensuring that specialised plant species such as fritillaries and cowslips become just a memory for most people. Even the humble hedgerow is under threat; nearly 400,000 kilometres have been pulled up since the end of World War II.

Road traffic

In an attempt to find a substitute for their traditional hunting sites, **barn owls** have taken to hunting on roadside verges. These, particularly motorway verges, are excellent places for small mammals. The majority are not sprayed or frequently cut and they are rarely disturbed by humans. As a result, they support a large number of voles, mice and shrews. When such a road goes through the territory of a barn owl, it will inevitably be exploited. The only problem is that owls do not understand about cars. All birds run a small risk each time they fly over the carriageway, but most are not above the road for long enough for the traffic to be a major threat. Owls suffer because they spend so much time hunting on the verge itself. Barn owls might look big and bulky but they weigh less than 500 grammes. Generally, birds ignore vehicles unless they are coming directly at them, and barn owls are no exception. They pay scant attention to motorway traffic

Another road casualty

speeding past them at 70 miles an hour. Then a monster lorry appears on the inside lane. The vacuum created by the passing of this giant sucks the helpless barn owl from the verge into the wake of the lorry and straight into the path of the vehicle behind.

In developed countries more barn owls are killed by traffic than by anything else. Up to 40 per cent of the chicks born in a single spring will be lying dead on the roads before winter. In one year alone, 5000 British barn owls might be killed by traffic. And the worst part is that there is little we can do about it. The Government can legislate against hunting and pollution and put protection orders on sensitive habitats, but it cannot ban traffic. There are almost 170,000 miles of made-up road in Britain and that figure will grow rather than dwindle. The only real solution would be to make roadside verges out of concrete, but that would be prohibitively expensive and ruin one of the safest small mammal habitats in the country.

Pesticides

The most far-reaching and damaging peril came with the introduction of a group of man-made pesticides known scientifically as 'chlorinated hydrocarbons', but known to users by brand names such as DDT and Dieldrin. These chemicals were first made in the nineteenth century and were widely used to fight human infections. Some time afterwards it was realised that they were also an extremely effective crop dressing that could protect seeds from the unwanted attention of insects, therefore increasing the yield. By today's standards these chemical compounds were marketed with indecent haste. Everyone knew that they worked, but few knew – or even seemed to have considered – what effects they would have on the environment.

In retrospect, these chemicals had two enormous drawbacks. The most obvious was that they were not selective – at high enough levels they will kill anything from a greenfly to a badger. The other was that the substances were highly stable. Modern pesticides only work for a relatively short time; they are lethal for long enough to deter the insects, but once the danger has passed they break down into harmless chemicals that no longer threaten any wildlife. DDT and its cousins remained deadly for months, even years, after their first use.

Farmers, in perfectly good faith, eagerly pounced on these new wonder-chemicals and liberally dosed their seeds before planting, to stop the wheat-bulb fly and other insects eating them and preventing germination. Countless tons were used on farmland all over the world. Within days, rain had washed the powerful pesticides into the soil to be carried into streams and rivers. Soon they spread and infiltrated ecosystems far from the original fields.

The agricultural results were dramatic – in some places insect damage was almost completely eliminated and it seemed that a miracle solution to an age-old problem had at last been found. The devastating side effects of these pesticides on other forms of life began to work equally rapidly, only it was a long time before they were noticed.

Any lethal, stable chemical that is used in such quantities *always* makes its presence felt throughout the surrounding habitat once it has become incorporated into the food chain. For example, a hungry wood mouse would have found a few grains of DDT-soaked wheat lying on the surface of a field. Within seconds the seeds were eaten and the mouse moved on in search of more. The seeds would be digested as usual, but the pesticide was stored inside the internal organs in its original form, just as lethal and dangerous as before, but at a level that was too low to harm the mouse. On the following night, while feeding, the mouse was picked off and eaten by a barn owl. That mouse would have been just one of several caught and, as they were all feeding in the same field, most would have been contaminated with small amounts of pesticide that the owl would then store inside its own body.

Individually, none of the mice contained enough to have much effect on the owl but once ten, twenty or thirty had been swallowed, the levels became high enough to kill by chemical poisoning. An untold number of owls, and other birds of prey, died through pesticide poisoning.

Even if they were not actually killed outright, the consequences of a high but non-lethal dose could be just as bad. This group of chemicals disrupts the nervous system, causing convulsions and loss of muscle control. The behaviour of many owls was changed by the effects of the poison; their hunting became erratic and much less successful; their senses were dulled and confused, and they became vulnerable to attack from larger predators.

Possibly the most unfortunate aspect of this chemical contamination was that it created an imbalance in the levels of sex hormones in birds. One of these, oestrogen, partially controls the flow of calcium within the female's body. The interference to this system reduced the ability in female birds of prey to produce calcium, the substance that makes up egg shell. The shells became so thin and weak that they smashed when the female gently sat to incubate, so instead of just one bird being killed outright by poison, a whole clutch was wiped out. Although owls were not as badly hit as other birds of prey, the introduction of these chemicals had a terrible effect on them and barn owls were particularly unlucky as they spend so much of their hunting time around farmland. The use of these chemicals was not finally banned in Britain until 1974, but even now they are still being used in some countries.

Government protection

I do not want this chapter to be full of doom and gloom, for that would not be a true picture. But it has to be said that, on balance, man has done more harm than good to owls. Some attempts have been made to redress the balance: for instance, in 1954 the first of several Acts was passed giving blanket protection to the majority of wild birds. This prevented people shooting, trapping or carrying out any of the other despicable practices that were once common. As part of this Act, there are lists (known as Schedules) of particularly vulnerable birds that are in need of special protection. On Schedule 1, the 'most protected' list, are **barn owls** and **snowy owls**. Not only must these species not be killed, they cannot even be disturbed when nesting.

Scientists that want to weigh chicks or pho-

tographers wishing to capture them on film must first obtain a licence from the relevant organisation. Without this piece of paper, anyone found close to the nest could be sentenced to prison or receive a hefty fine – or both. Like so many other sensible laws, this one is very difficult to enforce. Owls are still shot and trapped and fanatics are still willing to run the risk of prosecution to add new eggs to their collection – a sad wooden box of trays lined with cottonwool containing neat clutches of blown eggs that no one else can ever see because it is not supposed to exist.

The problems are not only confined to Britain. In some Mediterranean countries owls are hunted for sport, particularly the harmless **scops owl** as it passes through twice a year on migration. In the old part of Cairo market, freshly caught owls are on sale, stuffed into small wicker baskets. As few of the locals are interested in keeping non-productive pets, it is hard to see quite why they are bought. But I feel sure that the practice does not do the owls any favours.

Destruction of natural habitats

Problems left in the wake of continual destruction of rain forests have been well covered in the media over the past few years. The emphasis has rightly been on the issue of global warming, but as a result, only a little has been said about the loss of the resident

Snowy owl chick

wildlife. Rain forest dwellers are specialists at living in just one unique environment – they cannot exist anywhere else. With the forest disappearing, so is their future; and it is not only happening in the tropics.

The **spotted owl** of North America is one of the world's most threatened species. A quiet, inoffensive sort of bird that looks a bit like the tawny owl, it lives exclusively in a small area on the western side of the USA. It hunts flying squirrels, deer mice and other birds and mammals. Spotted owls are choosy when it comes to habitat; they like large tracts of undisturbed mature woodland – and so do logging companies but for very different reasons. In the states of Oregon and Washington there is an undeclared, unarmed war between conservationists and timber workers. The ecologists say that once a forest has been cleared it will take around 200 years for it to be renewed, and that is assuming the land is left completely alone. Obviously the spotted owls cannot wait that long for their home to reappear and if large-scale logging takes place they will be wiped out.

The loggers maintain that humans are more important than owls. Good jobs are hard to get in that area and commercial timber production is one of the more successful industries. This conflict, in some form, is taking place throughout the world, but seldom with such acrimony. It seemed that each time the conservationists managed to place a protection order on a vulnerable piece of wood-

Little owls can often be seen during the day, hunting for insects

land, there was often violent retaliation. Two spotted owls were beaten to death during a particularly nasty phase of the struggle; car stickers were seen in logging towns carrying the advice 'Save a logger – kill a spotted owl'. At the moment there are an estimated 4000 spotted owls left on earth. To me the issue is clear: wood can be grown virtually anywhere, spotted owls will not be so easy to replace.

In some places the forestry industry has considerably helped owls. New stands of young conifers make an excellent home for voles. As they scurry and feed in the grass between the low trees, they are irresistible to prowling owls. Once the fir trees get bigger, cutting out the light and scattering pine needles on the soil, nothing can grow on the ground beneath and the voles move on to richer pastures. Modern forestry is a skilled business and the professionals plan for the future. They want a steady supply of wood for the next fifty years, so planting is staggered and, at any one time, there should be trees of all ages in one forested area. Several of these plantations should be at just the right stage for both voles and owls; when the trees become too big, both species can simply move on to a more suitable site.

Whatever the specific problem, there is one unavoidable depressing equation: more people means less wildlife. In some ways the human fondness for towns and cities means that at least parts of the countryside are left in peace. Should the population ever be evenly spread over Britain, there would be no wild places left where animals could live.

Reintroduction through captive breeding

To be fair, people are working all over the world on various projects to ensure that owls do have a rosy long-term future. One of the better known, but still controversial, schemes is that of **reintroduction through captive breeding**. The idea is simple enough: where the habitat is suitable, but owls are missing, young birds are released and encouraged to breed in the hope that they will form the nucleus of a thriving colony. This approach does have its opponents, whose argument is that if the owls have left or died out, then there is a good reason why the area cannot support them.

I take the other view because so many animals are endangered through our direct interference. If a population of barn owls was wiped out because of the abuse of chemical pesticides, but the use of the pesticides is then stopped, the owls will slowly move back given enough time. Just because they are not present now does not mean that they can never live there again. If the habitat is capable of supporting barn owls, we can help the recolonisation by introducing fresh young blood. This is a job for experts and should not be carried out by anyone who feels that it would be 'nice' to have barn owls flying around the neighbourhood. At the moment it is perfectly legal to buy a pair of barn owls, drive home and release them into a suburban back garden, but 99.9 per cent of the time this would be a slow and unpleasant death sentence for both birds. Many countries are now considering the idea of licensing all release projects to ensure that the process is carried out correctly and without cruelty.

Adult owls that have spent all their lives in captivity are not mentally equipped for life in the wild. They lack the experience and 'field-cred' that is necessary for survival. Hunting is a learned skill and adult birds are usually too old to acquire it. Even if the birds are perfect candidates for release, the exact site must be chosen with great care. The habitat needs to be at low altitude, with hedges and copses to provide hunting grounds; there must be undisturbed old buildings or nest boxes where the birds can safely rear their young; the landowner should be sympathetic and extremely careful in his use of sprays, or preferably not use them at all. The list is long and each item has to be considered.

Reintroduction projects rely upon the fertility and productivity of captive pairs of barn owls. Under the right conditions they will breed like proverbial rabbits. As the size of the clutch is greatly affected by the availability of food, egg production should remain close to its theoretical maximum as long as the birds get a non-stop supply of mice from the keepers.

In a good year captive barn owls can have two or even three broods of young. The birds are left well alone during the nesting season – if they are continually disturbed by noisy humans, even the most well-balanced owls are quite likely to eat their chicks. To prevent this happening many breeders keep the owls in cages with solid sides, instead of the usual mesh, with a wire roof that gives the birds plenty of air and light but keeps them hidden from the world outside. The owls are provided with a strong wooden nest box, high inside the cage, with the entrance hole facing away from the door. They are then fed through a small trap-door. They can fly and feed normally but never come into contact with, or even see, their keeper.

If the chicks are to stand any chance of living in the wild, they have to be kept away from humans during the first few weeks of life. Most experts check on them just two or three times during this period and then only for a matter of seconds. There are more important matters to attend to at this stage – a release site must be picked. This involves a lot of leg-work, looking for an area that will meet all of the criteria that will give the birds the best possible start.

The most traumatic event comes when the young barn owls are ready to leave their nest box. This is a perfectly normal happening in the breeding cycle, only it usually takes place without the help of humans. This will be the first time that the chicks have seen any moving object other than their parents and they are absolutely terrified. They back into the corner, hiss and splutter and lash out with razor-sharp talons. Taking away the chicks and subjecting them to this ordeal might at first seem to be a heartless thing to do, but a healthy fear of man should be encouraged as it is a basic necessity for the survival of any wild animal.

It is at this stage that many aspiring enthusiasts make their critical mistake. If the owls have produced six chicks, they release them all at once and in the same place. This can be genetically fatal. Barn owls should only be released into a habitat where there are no other members of the species. This avoids direct competition for food and nest-sites. But the introduction of one by itself would be pointless as it could never breed. The owls should therefore go out in pairs. If, however, chicks from only one brood are released they will have no choice but to mate with their brothers and sisters. This is not terribly important in the first year, but with each successive spring it starts to become ever more dangerous. The intensive in-breeding of each new generation makes the owls more susceptible to physical deformities and infections. In the end, the entire population becomes so weak that it dies out and nothing has been accomplished.

To avoid this, all we need to do is release unrelated birds together, which is why anyone wishing to take part in a reintroduction scheme should not work alone, because inside a network it is possible to arrange for

Young owls should not be picked up – the parents will almost certainly be nearby

young owls to be exchanged ready for release. This alone gives them a far better chance of survival. The word 'release' gives the wrong impression of the process involved as it makes it sound as if we simply open up a cardboard box and the bird flies to its freedom and lives happily ever after. In reality it is a slow and repetitive job. Each exponent has his own way of doing things but they are all variations on the same theme.

For the first two weeks the young owls are locked into an abandoned barn or attic. This, it is hoped, will be where they eventually nest, although it doesn't always work out like that. The barn should be big enough for them to be able to move about freely; the two-week period gives them the chance to perfect their flying skills and learn that this is home, a safe place of retreat. Each day we take food to the barn, quickly check the birds and leave immediately. After fourteen days the windows or doors are opened and the young owls can fly free for the first time in their lives.

Although the owls now have the chance to hunt for themselves, it is important not to stop the food supply. I have taken food to a release site for up to three weeks after the grand opening while the birds master the techniques of search and kill. Each bird takes its own time but they gradually eat less of the food that I leave as they wean themselves on to prey that they have caught themselves. Finally there comes the day when they ignore my food totally – they have then become truly wild owls. After that, there is nothing left to do but hope.

Imprinting

Anyone who is serious about captive-breeding and release schemes has to keep a **detached attitude** towards the birds. It is tempting to handle the chicks and become fond of them but this is fraught with danger. It is important not only to keep the young birds in good physical health; their mental condition must also be safeguarded. This might sound odd but owls can become confused in the matter of their own identity. In the normal course of events, newly hatched owls are fed by their mother and they regularly see the male as he makes fleeting visits to deliver food. During their time in the nest they effectively learn what kind of animals they are by watching the adults. Once the nest has been left behind, the birds retain the early memories and for the rest of their lives this governs their attitude towards other members of their species.

The process of learning takes place during the first weeks of life; once their identity has been ingrained it **cannot be forgotten or changed**. To be candidates for release, the youngsters must be parent-reared, so that they grow up to be stable, well-balanced owls. If humans interfere, for whatever reason, the owls can become completely muddled. Although it is a complicated system that we don't fully understand, it seems that whatever feeds the young owl in the first critical weeks is automatically taken to be mother. Generally this is an excellent idea because the chicks know immediately where to look for food and protection.

Tawny owl chick at about three weeks old

If the owls are exclusively reared by a human, they grow up **believing themselves to be humans**. This is a very simplified way of explaining a phenomenon that zoologists call 'imprinting'. Many animals can experience it to some degree but geese and owls can be so thoroughly imprinted that it can often never be reversed. Responsible owl-breeders go to great lengths to avoid this situation but it can happen to even the most diligent. The depth of imprinting depends on the contact the owls have with the foster species while they are growing. Fully imprinted birds are so tame that they are virtually impossible to release. They become so reliant on us for food and company that they simply will not go. Of course it would be possible to drive out to some remote spot and throw the owl out to fend for itself but that would mean almost certain death. There is a move afoot to make this illegal under the Cruelty to Animals Act. In its way it is just as barbaric as locking up a dog and refusing to feed it.

Imprinting usually takes place when the mother dies or ignores her chicks and rapid action needs to be taken before any damage is done. This is the main reason why baby owls should not be rescued and looked after by novices, regardless of how well intentioned they might be. Young owls lying on the ground, peeping pitifully, have hardly ever been abandoned. More than likely they have fallen from the nest and have already been found by the parents. Although they will still

be fed, the young owls are highly vulnerable to attack by foxes, cats or a host of other predators. The best thing to do is *carefully* pick up the owl and put it into a nearby tree or bush. The female will soon find it. If you are still worried, have a look on the following day; only if the bird is weak or injured should it be 'looked after', and even then this should be done by an expert.

Many truly abandoned chicks can be found captive surrogate parents with ease. As owls cannot count, we just have to slip one or two extra chicks into a nest and the female does not notice that the size of her brood has suddenly increased. She is given more food, passes it on to the youngsters, and they finally grow up to be real owls with a healthy fear of man. The chicks must be paired up with parents of the **same species,** as the young owls can be imprinted by anything that moves. Bringing up a tawny owl as a barn owl is almost as bad as rearing it as a human, for when the breeding season arrives the changeling owl will not know what sort of partner to pick because of its unconventional past.

Chicks belonging to common species can quickly be farmed out to new homes but more unusual youngsters have a harder time. Some years ago I was presented with a very young and helpless eagle owl, which had been abandoned by its mother immediately after hatching. No suitable foster parents could be found so I had the job of hand-rearing it. At this stage the bird was just a bundle of off-white fluff. It was extremely untidy and looked as if it had been very badly knitted.

The young bird, which was named Rocky for no real reason at all, took up residence in a small cardboard box lined with old cotton rags that had to be changed daily. I do not want to be gratuitously gory, but the uncensored facts need to be told. I had to do all of those jobs that would normally be carried out by a true eagle owl mother. I had to cut up dead mice and carefully feed the owl with small slivers, as it was too weak to tear up the food itself. Eagle owls are mainly nocturnal but I had no intention of spending my nights dissecting mice and feeding bits to an ever-hungry owlet. It was fed five times a day, starting in the early morning and finishing around midnight. Each time I moved the owl called with an asthmatic wheeze, begging for food. This round ball of fluff was never really hungry, its call was simply a reflex action. In the wild it would have needed to outbid the other chicks whenever the parents were around. Its instinct demanded that begging signals should be sent out whenever mother (me) was about.

The owl spent much of the first ten days asleep and its eyes opened only when food was around. But they were worth waiting to see. Even at this tender age, Rocky showed the hypnotically brilliant eagle-owl orange irises that are the hallmark of the most impressive eyes on earth. Rocky adopted me

as her family without hesitation and wherever I went, somewhere nearby would be the cardboard box containing the growing monster. 'Ahhhh, it's a hamster,' was the comment that greeted us most of the time. And once, 'Oh no, it's a rat.' I never really understood these misguided identifications, but now I realise that not many people have had first-hand contact with baby owls. But even so . . . a *hamster*?

The sides of the box became increasingly untidy and tatty as Rocky pecked and pulled at the cardboard. She was born in May and by the warm days of August she had reached her maximum body weight of about four kilogrammes – Rocky is a big bird even by eagle-owl standards. She might have been full size, but she did not yet have her adult, brown/black feathers and was coated instead in a grubby-looking grey fluff with only tail and long flight feathers showing.

By now she was capable of eating anything that I gave her without help, but she was still a very insecure owl. She enjoyed going for walks in the garden and, although she couldn't fly, she stretched her wings and vigorously flapped without actually leaving the ground. The owl was intensely interested in creepy-crawlies and she would watch woodlice and spiders as they busily explored the long grass. She became so absorbed by the tiny creatures that she often did not notice me walk away. When she eventually realised that I had gone, a minor panic would

'Rocky,' the majestic eagle owl

set in. Using an inelegant and strange long-legged jog she would lope over the grass, displaying an unexpected burst of speed. With head down and fluffy, downy feathers trailing behind, she looked exactly like a respectable grandmother gathering up her petticoats for a swift sprint. For the next ten minutes she would not leave my heels, until another small beast demanded her attention.

By October she had matured into a fully developed eagle owl; there are few, if any, birds that are more handsome or majestic. I have been introduced to several imprinted owls but none has been quite like Rocky. She is content in the company of anyone but she does behave differently towards me. She dozes when unfamiliar people are around, completely unconcerned but always keeping half an eye on them in case they play some nasty trick on her. She seems to enjoy being stroked (although that is only my opinion), providing she can see who is doing it. But she gets very agitated when I'm not around and strangers are nearby.

Meeting an agitated *wild* eagle owl is one of life's experiences that should be avoided, for this is one of the most powerful and potentially dangerous birds on earth. They have few natural enemies; although golden eagles sometimes include males in their diet, a fully grown healthy female would probably be too much even for an eagle. But eagle owls have suffered more than any other European species at the hand of man. Until Victorian times they were officially classed as vermin and could be killed by anyone at any time. Several countries paid a bounty for each dead owl. This offer was too good to miss and by the turn of the century, eagle owls were on the verge of extinction over much of their range and still the killing continued. Nowadays governments are more sympathetic and eagle owls are legally protected in most of Europe.

Some countries, such as Germany, France and Sweden, have even started reintroduction programmes to replace their lost eagle owls and there are signs that these are helping the species to recover. However, eagle owls reproduce at a painfully slow rate and it could take years for them to recolonise lost ground. And time is against them. More of Europe's wild places are being tamed with each passing year, and the space and peace which these giant birds need are becoming increasingly rare.

At least my own is safe for the moment. Although I keep using the name 'Rocky', it is only for my convenience, as the owl does not recognise the word. However, her hearing is so acute that she can certainly identify my voice even when there are many other people talking. I always spend some time with her every day and before reaching her aviary, while still out of sight, I call her name. She always responds with a deep resonant 'oooo-hoooo'. If I call back, she replies, and this pattern can go on for some time. It is always I who gives up first. My conversations with the owl are long but intellectually undemanding. The word I call out is completely irrelevant as it is my voice that she knows, not what I say. I can stand in the garden and shout 'frozen cod' and she will still talk to me.

It is very rewarding to have a close relationship with such a special bird. When there is no one else about, she is a lot more playful with me. She sits as close as possible and preens my hair, just as she would a mate's feathers. Pulling the hair gently through her beak, she is maintaining a pair-bond with me in exactly the same way as she would with another eagle owl. She likes nibbling my ears and does so with great delicacy, my nose comes next, but she bites this so carefully that I can barely feel her touch.

I had Rocky in 1985. In eagle owl terms she is still a relative youngster; the world record age for the species is 68 years old, so she may outlive me. Rocky is now a seasoned traveller and when we go out there is no need to put her into a box; she sits on her own personal log in the back of the car, calmly watching the world go by. I once had a van for a short time, as it was more practical for owl-transportation. The experiment was a disaster, as I hadn't realised until then just how much Rocky liked to sightsee on our journeys. The van had no side windows, so she used to perch on the back of the passenger seat, with her head thrust forward so that she could peer through the windscreen. I felt quite at home driving along with an eagle owl sitting next to me, but other road-users seem to feel that the sight is unusual.

I now have a hatchback and she sits in the back happily looking out of the wide back window, but this creates its own problems. On motorways, drivers behind come indecently close to look at the giant owl. On more occasions than I can remember her photograph been taken by a passenger leaning out of the window while travelling at 70 miles an hour.

Once, I was pulled up by a police car. My road tax was up-to-date and I was well below the speed limit, so I couldn't work out why I had been stopped.

'Excuse me sir, could you tell me what kind of animal that is . . . in the back of your car?'

To the best of my knowledge owls are not mentioned anywhere in the Highway Code, but I was immediately convinced that her presence must contravene some obscure traffic regulation. I explained about Rocky and her history. The policeman asked about what she ate and so forth, until finally I had to find out if the police were going to take action against me. 'Oh no sir, I just wanted to know what it was so I could tell my wife when I got home.'

I feel sorriest of all for the children that see her. In my experience they are far more observant than their parents and, all too often, Mum and Dad sit in the front seat without noticing anything of the world they are speeding through. As their car overtakes

Rocky en route to a lecture

mine, however, the kids in the back seat frequently spot the owl. The effect is electric: they sit bolt upright, poke their bored parents in the back and point at the car. But by then my car is behind and the owl is hidden from view. Obviously I can't hear the conversation but it doesn't require much imagination to work it out. Children all over the country have probably been told off for telling fibs about a huge owl sitting in the back of a white hatchback on the motorway.

Traffic lights in busy towns are responsible for the most confusion. When cars have to wait for a minute or so while the lights are on red, passers-by often look in, only to catch a quick glimpse of the occupants before the lights change and the driver pulls away. Whenever Rocky is with me as we leave a busy junction, in my rear-view mirror I can see astonished and mystified pedestrians as they stand and look at the back of my disappearing car. Did they really see an owl? No, it couldn't have been, it must have been a funny-looking dog. Once, on the way to give a talk at a Conservation Trust meeting, I stopped to get some petrol on the outskirts of London. The cashier had obviously noticed Rocky but did not say anything until I had paid and turned to leave. 'Excuse me,' he said politely, 'did you know that you've got an owl in the back of your car?'

Having travelled extensively with Rocky, introducing her to what could have been intimidating surroundings, I really believed she was afraid of nothing, until the day I started to build a pool in the garden. After filling a wheelbarrow with soil, I went to empty it and walked past Rocky's outdoor aviary. She took one startled look at the wheelbarrow, dropped on to the floor and crouched as low as possible. Her ear tufts went down and her eyes became the narrowest slits. Each time I went past the aviary, Rocky went to ground and lay almost flat. At first I did not understand what was going on but after an hour it became obvious that she was frightened of the wheelbarrow. When most animals see a potential enemy they have the choice of either trying to negotiate their way out of the situation by using displays and bluff, or they can hide and escape – fighting is usually a last resort.

Displays are normally only used when the animal is confident of winning the conflict or if it is just not fast enough to make a getaway. Whenever I pushed a load of soil close to the eagle owl, she droppped to the floor and crouched in case the wheelbarrow saw her. To this day I cannot understand why she was so frightened – she has never been attacked by a wheelbarrow. In fact, she had never even seen one before then. We have since worked out that she does not like anything with wheels that does not make a noise. I suppose that even owls have the right to idiosyncratic phobias. Cars, lorries and tractors, no matter how big and noisy, are ignored by this awesomely powerful owl but silent, harmless bicy-

Despite my affection for Rocky, I would rather she had been able to grow up in the wild

cles and wheelbarrows reduce her to a quivering heap.

It should be stressed, however, that *no one* should ever intentionally try to imprint an owl. It is certainly the last thing that I want. Any bird that is humanised to this degree is doomed to life in captivity. The whole point of our rehabilitation centre, along with all others, is to make sure that injured and abandoned owls go back to the wild where they belong. Young owls should not be treated as pets; Rocky is the only imprinted bird I have and she's only like that because more suitable surrogate parents were not available. In retrospect, despite my affection for her, I would have preferred her to have grown up as a real eagle owl if it had been at all possible. But honesty compels me to say that Rocky is unique and the quality of my life would be measurably poorer without her.

It should also be emphasised that caring for any owl is a job for experts. Many people, for all the right reasons, want to care for birds that have been injured, but it takes a great deal of time and knowledge to do it properly. Most wild owls have to be force-fed for the first few days after their accident; even if they are physically capable of feeding themselves, the proximity of humans, strange food and unfamiliar surroundings all come together to intimidate them. Force-feeding sounds traumatic, and it can be for both owl and rescuer. This is not a task for the squeamish or inexperienced and it is always as well to remember that should anything go wrong, the owl will almost certainly die. By all means pick up injured owls, carefully wrapping a coat or old blanket loosely around the bird to prevent either party being hurt. Then, keeping it warm and quiet in a cardboard box, take it to a properly equipped rescue centre as soon as possible.

10 Owls in the 21st Century

Accurate insight into the behaviour and biology of any animal is always the first necessary step towards conserving it. We now know far more about the ecology of owls than we did twenty years ago but, even so, they stubbornly remain a remote group whose life style is largely shrouded in mystery. Due to their solitary lives and absolute need to find live food for themselves, owls are a difficult subject for conservation. At first it seems that there is little we can do to help their long-term survival, but although we may not be able to take many positive steps, we should try to eliminate the negative, man-made influences that threaten them.

As a group, owls do not face any particular imminent danger as do, for instance, the great whales. But there are some that stand on the brink of extinction and are likely soon to disappear into oblivion, if they have not already done so.

The **Madagascar red owl**, a member of the barn owl family, has been seen just once in the last sixty years.

The **Albertine owlet**, from central Africa, has been recorded just five times in history. The list could go on and it would probably include species that are completely doomed despite the fact that we are trying hard to save them. Humans now have to underwrite the future of all other species by acting *before* it is too late.

The biggest danger to owls, and most other wildlife, is habitat destruction. Ideally, there should be a planned global programme to care for sensitive environments but, as this is unlikely, everyone can help in some small way. Landowners should be persuaded to leave corners of their fields uncultivated so that small mammals can live and breed. New fields should be fenced with thick hedgerows instead of barbed wire; hedges are cheap, more effective than wire and last for years if they are trimmed and patched occasionally. They also provide homes for small creatures that cannot survive in open fields and some of these will undoubtedly fall prey to owls and other predators.

Urban 'green zones'

Tidiness and order are, ecologically, the curse of our times. A neatly mown lawn might look presentable but it is a desert to any animal larger than a worm or beetle. All over the country, people invest time, money and effort in keeping grass so short that nothing can live in it. If only we could interest councils, park authorities, cemetery committees and the managers of big business, they might become converted to the cause of practical conservation – they could even be coaxed into holding back with the industrial strimmers and ride-on mowers. We could encourage them to understand that at least some areas should be left completely untouched or, if managers of large-scale gardens cannot resist the temptation to cut grass, they could divide the land into sections and mow alternately, so that there would always be long undergrowth where voles and mice could live, wild flowers could grow and butterflies lay their eggs.

Within weeks these urban and suburban 'green zones' would attract wildlife. Towns would immediately become more vibrant and interesting for all who lived there, and we would be redressing the balance slightly, compensating just a little for the huge areas of wild habitat that are destroyed every single day, all over the world.

Tawny owl in nest box

Nest boxes

Positive action can be taken to encourage some owls and that is to provide suitable **nest boxes**. With the loss of so many traditional sites, finding safe breeding quarters will doubtless become more of a problem in the future. Not all owls will use boxes – the ground-nesters, for instance, have no need for them – but for some they are an ideal solution. **Little owls**, **barn owls** and particularly **tawnies** use them often enough to make the effort well worthwhile.

The boxes should be made of strong wood no less than 2 centimetres thick and should be treated with non-toxic preservative to make them last. The location of the box should be chosen with care; **tawny owls**, for example, prefer to nest in a coppice or woodland rather than in a single exposed tree. Each species requires its own design and there is little point in putting out a barn owl tray if there are none of these birds in the area. So do make sure there are owls about, or at least somewhere nearby, before reaching for the carpentry tools.

All boxes should be fixed **well above the ground** to stop the unwanted attention of cats, stoats and the numerous other predators that would make short work of defenceless young owls. The boxes should be **properly secured** since, in common with most birds, owls will not use 'wobbly' nests that might suddenly give way under the extra weight of

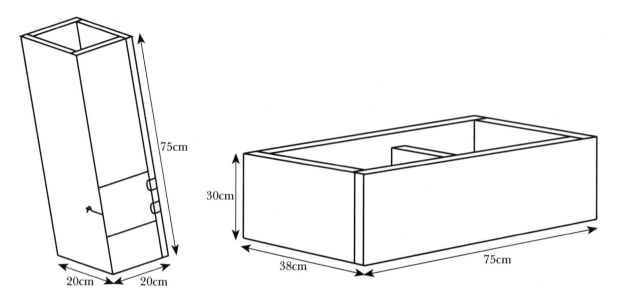

Tawny owl nest box. The box should be fixed to a tree at an angle of about 45º, with the hole facing upwards.

Barn owl nest box. This tray should be placed inside a dry, undisturbed building, close to an exit hole.

growing chicks. Ideally, the nests should be **north-facing** to prevent the chicks from cooking on hot spring days. There should also be several holes drilled through the bottom of the box to allow water to drain out.

Nest boxes need to be in position by the end of autumn to increase the chance of being used, as many owls choose their nests during the winter months. If the box is picked and becomes home to a pair of owls, it is safe to watch through binoculars from a distance, but the nest itself should be left well alone. Birds are very vulnerable at this time and any clumsy attempts to look at the chicks

could end in disaster. In the case of barn owls, an occupied nest is legally protected from human interference.

Some time ago, Scandinavian ornithologists began to be seriously concerned about the declining fortunes of the native **ural owl**, so they masterminded a wide-ranging and highly competent nest-box scheme that has completely reversed the trend and has set an almost perfect example to other aspiring conservationists. Boxes were first put out for these birds in 1960; today they breed in areas that lack natural nest holes, where previously they could not and their population has

Owls respond well to medical help and can recover from some terrible injuries

grown considerably as a result.

It is difficult to assist owls directly as they are at the top of the food chain. They have few enemies, they are strong, skilled and look absolutely secure perched at the peak of their ecosystems. The environment and its animals seem to be at the mercy of the biggest predators but, in fact, it is a well-matched balance and any significant changes in the habitat can have catastrophic effects on the animals at the top of the chain. Without a strong system to support them they cannot survive. If our great-grandchildren are going to have the chance of watching these almost mystical birds, we must start now by working to guarantee the future of owls' habitats.

Whenever man competes with animals for land use, humans win – always. It is fair to say that anything that is good for owls will be good for wildlife in general. We should all bear in mind that man is just another species of animal that has the same basic requirements as every other creature. If we continue to pollute air and water, cut down ancient forests that stabilise our atmosphere and help control the earth's temperature, then everything will eventually die, including us.

Most owls are tough and adaptable survivors, as can be seen from their geographical range and the diversity of habitats in which they live. But even owls cannot keep pace with the speed at which humans are changing the world. They need our assistance. Everyone can help to some degree by joining one of the many societies that are fighting to keep parts of the countryside wild and untouched. The Royal Society for the Protection of Birds, the Worldwide Fund for Nature and the County Conservation Trusts are just some of the groups that work tirelessly, in the face of mounting odds, to try to stop the relentless devastation of wilderness areas; but it is an uphill struggle and they need all the help they can get. Conservation needs both the political and financial weight of public support to succeed; so plant a tree or two, join a conservation group, ease up a little on the garden pesticides, and **act now**. Its the least you can do not only for owls but for all wildlife, and ultimately humans everywhere.

Photographic Notes

Some of the photographs in this book have been slowly accumulated over the years that I have worked with owls, while others were taken to illustrate specific points in the text. The nocturnal portraits were taken using a very old and battered **Braun** flash system with two heads that were always placed well away from the camera to avoid the dreaded 'red-eye' syndrome that spoils so many pictures. When photographing owls, or any other nocturnal animal, it is essential that the flash should *not* be used on top of the camera.

The high-speed photographs were taken by the owls themselves. They fly through an invisible beam of infra-red light that, when broken, triggers a motor-driven camera. When the shutter opens, three flash heads go off simultaneously at 1/20,000th second and freeze all movement. The whole thing takes less than 1/40th second from start to finish, the camera then winds on automatically and is ready to take another shot. This is a complicated system that, on average, gives a success rate of less than one in thirty.

The camera is focused on the centre of the beam, but the owl can fire the camera by flying through at any point. This produces photographs with just a pair of legs hanging down from the top of the frame, or the edge of a wing creeping into one side. Most of my high-speed pictures are thrown straight into the bin, but out of every three or four films there is usually at least one that is well worth all the effort. The high-speed flash unit is portable and powered by a huge battery. The control box runs at 2000 volts and needs to be treated with respect. The system generates so much heat that it can only be used once every three minutes. All of the flight pictures were taken on a **Bronica** with 150mm lens, using **Fujichrome 50** film.

The majority of the daylight pictures were taken on a **Pentax** with a 400mm lens, with the exception of the saw-whet owl, and a sturdy **Benbo** tripod was used for every picture. All 35mm colour photographs were taken on **Kodachrome 64**.

Owls are remarkably photogenic subjects.

Tawny owl landing

They make perfect models – the hard part is getting the camera into the right place to photograph them. Wildlife photography is a matter of knowing where to find the subject and how to approach it. There are no cast-iron rules, bar one. THE WELFARE OF THE SUBJECT MUST ALWAYS COME FIRST. A careless photographer can drive a bird out of its habitat or even make it abandon its nest. No picture is worth that. Wildlife photographs should be a tool for conservation, a way of showing the world that these animals exist and should be cared for – before it is too late to help.

Bibliography

Bunn, D. S., Warburton, A. B., and Wilson, R. D. S., *The Barn Owl*, Poyser, 1983.

Burton, John (ed.), *Owls of the World*, Peter Lowe, 1984.

Holmgren, Virginia, *Owls in Folklore and Natural History,* Capra Press, 1988.

Hosking, Eric, and Flegg, Jim, *Eric Hosking's Owls*, Mermaid, 1982.

Johnsgard, Paul, *North American Owls: Biology and Natural History*, Smithsonian Institution Press (USA), 1988.

Kemp, Alan, *Owls of Southern Africa,* New Holland, 1988.

Maslow, Jonathan Evan, *The Owl Papers*, Penguin, 1983.

Mead, Chris, *Owls*, Whittet Books, 1987.

Mikkola, Heimo, *Owls of Europe*, Poyser, 1983.

Nero, Robert, *The Great Grey Owl: Phantom of the Northern Forest*, Smithsonian Institution Press, 1980.

Shawyer, C., *The Barn Owl in the British Isles*, Hawk Trust, 1987.

Sparks, John, and Soper, Tony, *Owls*, David & Charles, 1989.

Taylor, Iain, *The Barn Owl*, Shire Natural History, 1989.

Toops, Connie, *The Enchanting Owl*, Swan Hill Press, 1990.

Voous, Karel, *Owls of the Northern Hemisphere*, Collins, 1988.

Useful Addresses

British Trust for Conservation Volunteers
36 St Mary's Street, Wallingford, Oxfordshire
OX10 OEU.
A charity that organises groups of volunteers to
carry out practical management work on nature
reserves and other important habitats.

Hawk & Owl Trust
c/o Zoological Society of London, Regent's Park,
London NW1 4RY.
Registered charity dedicated to the conservation
and study of owls and birds of prey. Organises
surveys, advises landowners on habitat management, publishes reports and educational material.

Owl Study Group
c/o British Trust for Ornithology, The Nunnery,
Nunnery Place, Thetford, Norfolk IP24 2PU.
A group that keeps its members in touch with
up-to-date research projects concerning owls.

Royal Society for Nature Conservation (RSNC)
The Green, Witham Park, Lincoln LN5 7JR.
The advisory body that co-ordinates the work of
County Conservation Trusts. Has a junior section
known as WATCH, geared to interest children in
wildlife and conservation.

Royal Society for the Protection of Birds (RSPB)
The Lodge, Sandy, Bedfordshire SG19 2DL.
Europe's largest voluntary wildlife conservation
body. A registered charity established to protect
wild birds and their habitats both in Britain and
abroad.

Woodland Trust
Autumn Park, Dysart Road, Grantham,
Lincolnshire NG31 6LL.
A charity devoted to safeguarding the native
woodlands of Britain. Manages more than 400
woodlands, to the benefit of the trees and wildlife.

INDEX